flipped eye publishing
with
African Writers Abroad

dance the guns to silence

100 poems for Ken Saro-Wiwa

foreword by Ken Wiwa

simple words rendered sublime

dance the guns to silence - 100 poems for Ken Saro-Wiwa

flipped eye publishing limited
www.flippedeye.net

'Flight' by Matthew Caley is taken from *The Scene Of My Former Triumph* published by Wrecking Ball Press.

'This is How' by Fred Bahnson is forthcoming in the journal *Rock and Sling: A journal of Literature, Art and Faith*, Volume 2 Issue 2.

'A Candle for Ken Saro-Wiwa' by Stewart Brown is taken from *Elsewhere* and reproduced with kind permission of Peepal Tree Press.

'The Truce' by Alison Fell is taken from *Dreams, Like Heretics: New and Selected Poems* published by Serpents Tail, 1997

(c) 'New World Hawdah' by Linton Kwesi Johnson reproduced by kind permission of LKJ Music Publishers Ltd. First published in *'Mi Revalueshanary Fren: Selected Poems'* by Linton Kwesi Johnson (Penguin: London, 2002)

'The Agonist' by Ogaga Ifowodo is extracted from *The Oil Lamp* published by Africa World Press, 2005 and first appeared in The Massachusetts Review, vol. XLII, No. 2 (Summer 2002)

'The Man Who Asked Tall Questions' by Niyi Osundare is taken from *Ogoni's Agonies: Ken Saro-Wiwa and the Crisis in Nigeria.* ed. By Abdul Rasheed Na'Allah and published by Africa World Press. The extract here is a modified version.

'Wallace' by Andrew McCallum is from *The Wallace Muse* and reproduced here with kind permission of Luath Press Ltd.

'Famine Injection' by Mutabaruka is taken from *Mutabaruka: the next poems* and is reproduced with kind permission of Paul Issa Publications, 2005

'Landowners' by Pascale Petit is taken from *The Zoo Father* reproduced here with kind permission of Seren, 2001.

'Letter to My Nephew' by Mukoma Wa Ngugi first appeared in *Brick Magazine*, 2001.

'Voice' by Allene Rasmussen Nichols first appeared in *Fait Accomplit* in the Spring of 2004.

'Nine' by James Robertson first appeared in *The Dark Horse* issue no. 7 in 1998.

'The Buddhas of Bamiyan' by Eva Salzman is taken from *Double Crossing: New & Selected Poems* and is reproduced here with kind permission of Bloodaxe.

'Content Metamorphosis.' by Yuyutsu RD Sharma is taken from *The Lake Fewa and a Horse* (Poems) 2004 published by Nirala Publishers.

Editors: Nii Ayikwei Parkes & Kadija Sesay
Editorial Advisor: Jack Mapanje

Printed and bound in the United Kingdom

ISBN: 1-905233-01-9

dance the guns to silence

100 poems for Ken Saro-Wiwa

With thanks to:
Arts Council England, London whose funding has supported the publishing of this book and the arrangement of the launch reading organised by African Writers Abroad on 10 November 2005 in London as part of the Remember Saro-Wiwa campaign, and further readings in New York and Washington, DC. To American PEN Center and TransAfrica Forum's support and collaboration to launch the book in New York and Washington, DC respectively; Rachel E. Griffiths and Kamilah Aisha Moon who read everyone one of the 600 or more poems submitted from around the world for inclusion in this anthology; Jack Mapanje, our editorial advisor, for his time, encouragement, advice and suggestions; Theodore Harris who graciously granted us permission to use his collage, We Wear Our Flesh Like Flames for the cover; Platform for their support and encouragement and initiating the Remember Saro-Wiwa Campaign; Peepal Tree Press whose support gave Kadija the flexibility to just get on and do what needed to be done to get this book out in time; all of the poets who submitted their poems, and in doing so, showed their commitment, honour and respect to the writer and activist Ken Saro-Wiwa, his colleagues, their work and ideals and lastly and most importantly, to all of the poets in this book who have made this book a living memorial.

The Editors,
London
2005

Foreword

"I've lived six or seven lives," my father once wrote to me from his detention cell.

I've seen him described variously as writer, poet or environmentalist to confirm at least three of those lives. Deep down, I think he would have liked to have been remembered as a writer, but sometimes I wonder whether the poet, the writer and the environmentalist are not one and the same? The writer is his cause, as he was fond of saying. His pen was sharper than a bullet and whether it was a full-scale war of the novel, the field battle of journalism or the guerrilla combat of the poem, he used all the tools of his trade. Yet for all those six or seven lives, Ken was not really a poet; still it is the poem that, for me, best articulates the heroic narrative of Ken Saro-Wiwa and here; in elegies that range from the fields of Ogoni, to the streets of Baghdad and the drilling fields of the Arctic; is a collection that pays tribute to the testament of the writer and his cause.

The struggle continues but to be the inspiration of the fighting words of your fellow poet, is the best story a writer can leave behind.

Ken Wiwa

On the fifth attempt it worked

- Daniel
- Felix
- Nordu
- Paul

- The Doctor
- Saturday
- Barribor
- John
- And Ken

Bori Camp, Port Harcourt, 10th November, 1995

(from *In The Ear of the Shell* by Gareth Evans)

Contents

Dance
Ken Saro-Wiwa

Dance your anger and your joys
Dance the military guns to silence
Dance their dumb laws to the dump
Dance oppression and injustice to death
Dance the end of Shell's ecological war of 30 years
Dance my people for we have seen tomorrow
and there is an Ogoni star in the sky

Biography of Ken Saro-Wiwa

Ken Saro-Wiwa's career spanned teaching, business, government administration, writing and political leadership. It was these last two for which he became renowned, and eventually murdered. His writings included satirical novels, newspaper columns, children's tales, folk tales and the popular television play Basi & Co. - a long-running series of over 150 episodes. For many Africans, he epitomised the freedom fighter.

From 1990, Ken Saro-Wiwa led a movement in Ogoni for social and ecological justice. He used his writing and his boundless energy to unite the Ogoni behind a call for greater autonomy within the Nigerian Federation, access to oil revenues for the development of Ogoni, the right to protect Ogoni from ecological devastation and the right to preserve the Ogoni language. In November 1990, the Ogoni Bill of Rights was signed by most Ogoni chiefs and leaders. The Movement for the Survival of the Ogoni People (MOSOP) was also founded to pursue this agenda along the principles of non-violence.

Throughout the early 1990s Ken campaigned vigorously for MOSOP as its President and travelled internationally to bring the cause to the attention of the United Nations and the international community. In 1994, the government arrested Saro-Wiwa and thirteen other Ogoni accusing them of the murder of four Ogoni chiefs during rioting in May 1994 even though the evidence suggested that Saro-Wiwa and others were many miles away from the scene of the crime. On 30 October 1995, following a show trial denounced by international observers, Ken Saro-Wiwa and eight of the accused were found guilty and sentenced to hang. Despite massive international outcry, the sentence was carried out on 10 November 1995. After their execution, they became known as The Ogoni 9 and the campaign to clear their name continues.

Biography of Ken Saro-Wiwa

Author Biographies

Chris Abani's latest novel *GraceLand* received the Hemingway/ PEN prize and was a finalist for the Commonwealth Prize Africa Region. See www.chrisabani.com

Montserrat Abelló, poet and translator, has published several books of poetry including the award winning *Dins l'Esfera del Temps*. In 1988 she was awarded the 'Creu de Sant Jordi' for her poetical work, feminist work and translations.

Peter Kayode Adegbie is a PhD Creative Writing student at Newcastle University, Newcastle upon Tyne, England.

Opal Palmer Adisa often lives inside her head, but manages to be in the world, sometimes. Check out her *Caribbean Passion*. Visit her at www.opalwriters.com

Nedda G. de Anhalt is Vice President for PEN Mexico, born in Havana Cuba, Mexican since 1967. An MA in Latin American Studies, Nedda has been published in more than twenty books.

Fred Bahnson's writing has appeared in *Fugue, Rock & Sling, Sojourners,* and *Pilgrimage* (forthcoming). He grew up in Jos, Nigeria, and now farms in North Carolina, U.S. ffbahnson@hotmail.com

Ismail Bala is a lecturer in English at Bayero University, Kano, Nigeria. He has published poems in numerous national and international anthologies and journals.

Amiri Baraka is the author of over 40 books of essays, poems, drama, music history and criticism. His controversial poem *Somebody Blew Up America* was written whilst he was Poet Laureate of New Jersey. He is married to Amina Baraka. www.amiribaraka.com

Nnimmo Bassey is an architect, environmental rights activist and a writer. He has published four volumes of poetry.

Iolanda Bonet is a writer. She works as Co-ordinator of Foreigners Educational Programs. She has published books for children and adults.

Carmen Borja has a doctor's degree in Spanish Literature and has lived in Barcelona since 1978. Her latest published work is *Libro de la Torre* (El Bardo, Barcelona, 2000).

Kamau Brathwaite is a Bajan poet and essayist and Professor of Comparitive Literature at NYU. His latest poetry book is *Born to Slow Horses*, produced in his signature underground Sycoraxian style.

Stewart Brown is currently Director of CWAS, Birmingham University. Editor, with Mark McWatt, of *The Oxford Book of Caribbean Verse* (2005). His selected poems, *Elsewhere* is published by Peepal Tree Press. s.brown@bham.ac.uk

Matthew Caley's second collection *The Scene Of My Former Triumph* (Wrecking Ball) is out now. Debut collection, *Thirst* (Slow Dancer, 1999) was a Forward Prize nomination.

Syl Cheney-Coker is a Sierra Leonean poet and novelist. Winner of both the Africa Best Book Commonwealth Writer's Prize and the Commonwealth Short Story Prize. A new poetry collection, *Stone Child* is with Bloodaxe .

Staceyann Chin: Jamaican, resident of Brooklyn. Nuyorican Poets' Café, one-woman shows Off-Broadway, poetry performances – around the globe—co-writer/performer in the Tony award winning 'Russell Simmons Def Poetry Jam on Broadway'. www.chinpoet.com

George Elliott Clarke is an Africadian (African-Nova Scotian) poet, librettist, novelist, and essayist. His latest book is the acclaimed novel, *George & Rue.*

Merle Collins is a Grenadian born poet, Professor of English and Comparitive literature at the University of Maryland. Her latest collection is *Lady in a Boat* (Peepal Tree Press).

Jayne Cortez is the author of ten books of poetry, performer with her band on nine recordings, and president of the Organization of Women Writers of Africa. www.jayne cortez.com

Paolo da Costa was born in Angola, raised in Portugal and presently lives on the West Coast of Canada. www.paulodacosta.com

Fred D'Aguiar is a poet and novelist and playwright and Professor of English at Virginia Tech. His latest novel is *Bethany Bettany* www.fred.d'aguiar.com

Kwame Dawes is poet, novelist, actor, musician, playwright and critic. He has several books published by Peepal Tree Press and is currently Professor of English at the University of South Carolina. www.kwamedawes.com

Daphne de Jong is a New Zealander. She is published worldwide in poetry and prose, and has won several awards including New Zealand's most prestigious short story prize, the Katherine Mansfield Short Story Award. www.daphneclair.com daphne@daphneclair.com

David Eggleton is a New Zealand poet, writer, and journalist of Polynesian and European descent who has been publishing and performing for over twenty years.

Zena Edwards is a "Tottenham poet/singer/writer, quoted as being one of the most refreshing, ever-developing voices in the UK, has poems published in several anthologies and performs her work internationally."

Jeanne Ellin is a poet, counsellor, reminiscence worker and storyteller. Her first a collection of poetry is *Who Asked the Butterfly?* (Peepal Tree Press). She currently holds a writer in residence post in Aberdeen, Scotland.

Martín Espada is an award winning poet with seven collections. The latest is *Alabanza: New and Selected Poems (1982-2002)*. He is a Professor at University of Massachusetts-Amherst, teaching creative writing and the work of Pablo Neruda.

Gareth Evans is a writer and film curator. He writes for *Time Out* and edits the film magazine *Vertigo* (www.vertigomagazine.co.uk). If you would like to receive his full poem, please email gareth@drifting.demon.co.uk

Alison Fell has published seven novels and four collections of poetry, the latest of which is *Liteyear* (Smokestack Books, 2005).

Chrissie Gittens is a poet and playwright. She has spent time in refugee camps on the Thai-Burma border. These poems are from her first collection *Armature* (Arc, 2003).

Lorri Neilsen Glenn is the author of several books including *All the Perfect Disguises* (Broken Jaw, 2003). She is the Poet Laureate of Halifax for 2005-2009.

Rachel Eliza Griffiths is a MFA candidate at Sarah Lawrence College. She lives in New York City.

Helon Habila is the author of the novel *Waiting for an Angel* (Hamish Hamilton). He is a PhD Creative Writing student at the University of East Anglia, England.

Nathalie Handal's recent publications: *Spell* (CD) and *The Lives of Rain,* Shortlisted for The Agnes Lynch Starrett Poetry Prize. She is currently working on the film, 'Gibran'.

Choman Hardi started writing poetry in Kurdish and gradually switched to English five years ago. *Life for Us,* her first English collection was published by Bloodaxe in 2004.

Theodore A. Harris is a visual artist, poet, published in many journals and anthologies. He has co-authored *Our Flesh of Flames: Captions by Amiri Baraka and Collages by Theodore A. Harris.*

Randall Horton is from Birmingham, Alabama. He is currently a candidate for an MFA in Creative Writing in Poetry at Chicago State University.

Allan Kolski Horwitz is a South African poet and member of the performance poetry group, Botsotso Jesters that sets out to create a mosaic of South African life.

Chenjerai Hove is a Zimbabwean poet and novelist, winner of the Noma Award for Publishing in Africa, 1989, for his novel, *Bones*.

Ogaga Ifowodo, a lawyer, holds an MFA from Cornell University. He has previously published *Homeland & Other Poems* (1998), *Madiba* (2003), and *The Oil Lamp* (2005). He can be reached at oei3@cornell.edu

Linton Kwesi Johnson is a poet and recording artist. He has published five collections of poetry and released 15 albums. Website: www.lkjrecords.com

Kiguli, Nalugwa Susan is a Ugandan Poet currently teaching at Makerere University, Uganda. She is also the present chairperson for FEMRITE (Uganda Women Writers' Association).

Monica Kidd is the author of *Beatrice* (Turnstone Press, 2001) and *The Momentum of Red* (Raincoat Books, 2004). She lives in St. John's, Newfoundland, where she attends medical school.

Lucia Sehui Kim was born in Seoul, South Korea and currently lives in New York City. At this time she is pursuing her Masters in Fine Arts degree at Sarah Lawrence College. luciakim@gmail.com

Jerome Kugan is a writer musician based in Kuala Lumpur, Malaysia.

Yael Langella is a poet, photographer and translator. She has exhibited in galleries from Catalonia, Spain, Israel and France. She also writes presentations for painters and sculptors exhibits.

Josef Lesser lives with his wife on the mid-north coast of New South Wales Australia. "I believe poems are as distinct from one person to another as fingerprints." jmlesser@ozemail.com.au

Danson Kahyana teaches Literature at Makerere University, Kampala. He is the General Secretary of Ugandan P.E.N.

John Lyons Trinidadian poet and painter; Wind Rush Arts Achiever 2003; twice winner, national Peterloo Poetry Competition; three poetry collections published and has works in numerous anthologies.

Andrew McCallum lives and works in the Scottish Borders. A libertarian in the Scots tradition, his poetic mentor is the great modernist poet, Hugh MacDiarmid.

Sarah Maguire is the founder and director of The Poetry Translation Centre at SOAS. She's published three collections of poetry, most recently *The Florist's at Midnight* (Cape, 2001).

Lisa Suhair Majaj, a Palestinian-American writer living in Cyprus, has published, most recently, in *World Literature Today* and *Banipal: Magazine of Modern Arab Literature.* lmajaj@cytanet.com.cy

Jack Mapanje is the author of several poetry collections. He currently teaches memoir writing and Literature of Incarceration at Newcastle University, England.

Tony Medina is the author of twelve books for adults and children. He is currently Assistant Professor of Creative Writing at Howard University, Washington DC.

E. Ethelbert Miller is a literary activist, author and board chair of the Institute for Policy Studies. His latest book is, *How We Sleep On The Nights We Don't Make Love*. www.eethelbertmiller.com Emiller698@aol.com **The format of his poem has been adapted slightly to fit this volume.*

Anna Mioduchowska is a poet, translator and author of stories, essays and book reviews. *In-Between Season*, a poetry collection, was published by Rowan.

Kamilah Aisha Moon is a Cave Canem alumna whose work has been featured in *Mosaic, Bittersweet, The Black Arts Quarterly, bum rush the page, Warpland, OBSIDIAN III, Toward the Livable City* and *SABLE LitMag.* Moonpoet1@yahoo.com

Simon Murray writes short stories, poetry, comedy and dabbles in art. He once worked in advertising and is now writing a novel to redeem his soul. www.simurrai.com email: info@simurrai.com

Walusako A. Mwalilini from Malawi, is a graduate of Columbia University and the Johns Hopkins University. He works in Washington, D.C. mwalilino@aol.com.

Mutabaruka is a Jamaican Dub Poet and broadcaster. His latest collection is *Mutabaruka : the first poems* and *Mutabaruka : the next poems,* in one volume. www.mutabaruka.com

Mukoma Wa Ngugi is a Kenyan poet who authored *Conversing with Africa: Politics of Change,* the forthcoming *A Malignant History: Looking at America* and is the Coordinator of the Toward an Africa without Borders Organization.

Allene Rasmussen Nichols is a playwright and poet. She lives in Arlington, Texas and teaches English and drama at Gateway School. allenen@pobox.com

Odia Ofeimun is the president of the Association of Nigerian Authors. His major poetry collections are *The Poet Lied, A Handle for the Flutist and Other Poems,* and *Under African Skies.*

Ogo Ogbata (pronounced '*or-gore or-gbata*') has presented poetry and fiction for BBC Radio. Her first novel *Egg-Larva-Pupa-Woman* is soon to be published in the UK. Visit: www.ogo-ogbata.com

Tolu Ogunlesi, 23, is the author of a collection of poetry *Listen to the Geckos Singing From a Balcony* (Bewrite Books, UK, 2004). to4ogunlesi@yahoo.com

Omolola Ijeoma Ogunyemi is an Assistant Professor at Harvard Medical School. Her poetry has appeared or is forthcoming in the *Massachusetts Review* and *Wasafiri.* ijeoma@yahoo.com

Tanure Ojaide is a Nigerian poet currently teaching at the University of North Carolina at Charlotte. Tojaide@email.uncc.edu

Ewuare Osayande, political activist and author of several books including *Blood Luxury* (Africa World Press), is co-founder of POWER (People Organized Working to Eradicate Racism). www.osayande.org

Niyi Osundare is a poet, dramatist, critic, essayist, and media columnist. Until recently, he was Professor of English at the University of New Orleans. He is currently at Franklin Pierce College, in New Hampshire.

Ruth Padel has won the National Poetry Competition and published six collections, most recently *The Soho Leopard* (Chatto & Windus), a Poetry Book Society Choice.www.ruthpadel.com

Nii Ayikwei Parkes (co-editor) is a Ghanaian writer, editor, social and literary commentator. He set up The Writers' Fund to support creative writing initiatives in Ghana. www.thewritersfund.org

Pascale Petit's latest collections are *The Huntress* (Seren, 2005), and *The Wounded Deer* (Smith Doorstop, 2005). In 2004 she was selected as a Next Generation Poet. pascalepetit@btinternet.com

Mario Petrucci, ecologist, physicist, literary innovator. First resident poet at the Imperial War Museum and BBC Radio 3 *Heavy Water* (Enitharmon) won the coveted Arvon Prize. http://mariopetrucci.port5.com

Geoffrey Philp, a Jamaican writer, has four poetry collections , the author of *Twelve Poems and A Story for Christmas* and the novel, *Benjamin, my son*. He lives in Miami, Florida. www.geoffreyphilp.com | geoffreyphilp@aol.com

Stella Pierides was born in Athens, Greece. She lives in Munich and London. She writes poetry and prose and is a member of English PEN and Munich Writers. www.stellapierides.com

Kevin Powell is a political activist and an award-winning writer. The author or editor of six books, his next, *Someday We'll All Be Free*, is a collection of essays on freedom and democracy (Random House, 2006)

Susan Richardson is a poet, travel writer and tutor of creative writing based in Wales. For more information about her work, please visit www.susanrichardsonwriter.co.uk

Angel V. Shannon is the author of *...And Then ThereWere Butterflies* (2004). She balances a career in medicine with writing, mothering, and working for social change. www.angelvshannon.typepad.com | avshann@yahoo.com

James Robertson is a widely published Scottish poet and author of the novels *The Fanatic* and *Joseph Knight*. james@kettillonia.co.uk

Suhayl Saadi is a Novelist, stage/ radio dramatist (UK). *Psychoraag* (2004) shortlisted major fiction prize. Appears internationally. Worked (ed.) with Brink and Tutu on *'Freedom Spring'* (2005). www.suhaylsaadi.com

Kalamu ya Salaam is an editor/writer, filmmaker, producer and arts administrator. His latest spoken word CD is *My Story, My Song*. He is currently co-ordinating the Listen to the People project. www.nathanielturner.com/bio.htm

Eva Salzman: Originally from Brooklyn, Eva Salzman was Delegate for Writers-in-Exile NYC, at PEN International's Writers-in-Prison Barcelona Conference 2005. Her *Double Crossing: New & Selected Poems* (Bloodaxe) was a Poetry Book Society Recommendation

Sonia Sanchez is a poet, mother, activist, professor. She is author of 17 books including *Does Your House Have Lions?* and *Shake Loose My Skin.*

Kadija Sesay is a literary activist, founder publisher of the exquisitely beautiful LitMag *LitMag,* and General Secretary of African Writers Abroad (PEN) Centre. www.sablelitmag.org

Yuyutsu R.D. Sharma is a recipient of fellowships from The Rockefeller Foundation. He has published five poetry collections. A Punjab-born, Kathmandu-based poet, he edits the literary magazine *Pratik*. Website: www.yuyutsu.de

Lola Shoneyin is a Nigerian poet and author of two poetry collections, her latest, *And All This Time I Was Sitting On An Egg.*

John Siddique - Author of *The Prize* (The Rialto,) and editor of *Transparency"* (Crocus Books,) loves salty food, and people who can listen whilst talking. www.johnsiddique.co.uk

Lemn Sissay writes books of poetry, plays and makes broadcasts for BBC radio. He reads his poetry on stages around the world. www.lemnsissay.com

Goran Simic is a Bosnian/Canadian poet, essayist, playwright and fiction writer. www.angelfire.com/poetry/goransimic/

Rommi Smith, poet and playwright works to fuse spoken word and music. Currently writer in residence for BBC Radio 3's Africa Season, her forthcoming second collection is *Mornings and Midnights*. www.rommi-smith.co.uk

Sharan Strange is the author of *Ash* (Beacon Press). She lives in Atlanta, Georgia where she teaches at Spelman College.

Veronique Tadjo is a writer and artist from Cote d'Ivoire. A former lecturer at the University of Abidjan, her latest novel, *Reine Pokou* is published by Actes Sud in Paris.

Margo Tamez (Lipan-Apache) authored *Naked Wanting* (University Arizona Press), *Alleys & Allies* (Saddletramp Press). New collections are forthcoming (2006) from University of Arizona & Kore Presses. mtamez@wsu.edu

Heather Taylor is a Canadian poet, playwright & educator. She is published throughout Europe and North America with her collection *Horizon & Back* Tall-Lighthouse (October 2005). www.heathertaylor.co.uk | info@heathertaylor.co.uk

Steve Tasane - from Cheltenham Festival of Literature to Ken Livingstone's RISE Festival, by way of residencies including Hamleys Toy Shop and tours of music venues, Tasane bridges radicalism and populism with funky polemic and savage satire.

Carles Torner (Barcelona, 1963) is a Catalan poet, essayist and novelist, and has been committed for years to PEN International. This poem is from the book. *Life Afterwards* (1998, National Critics Award). ctorner@llull.com

Gustavo Alberto Garcia Vaca is a poet and visual artist. His writing is published in various books and his artwork is exhibited internationally. His website is www.chamanvision.com

Cyril Wong is the author of four poetry collections, including *Unmarked Treasure,* in Singapore. For more information visit cyrilwong.com.

Wong Ting Hway is a Singaporean doctor. She has worked with various humanitarian organisations, including Médecins Sans Frontières.wongtinghway@yahoo.com

Kabura Zakama, a veterinarian and a development worker, writes simple poetry that has a wide appeal. He won the 1999 ANA Poetry Prize.

Benjamin Zephaniah is a poet, novelist and playwright. He has published several poetry collections, written successful novels for young people and travels around the world performing his poetry. www.benjaminzephaniah.com

Editors & Cover Artist

JACK MAPANJE (Editorial Advisor): Jack Mapanje is a distinguished Malawian poet, linguist, editor and scholar. Formerly head of Department of English at Chancellor College, University of Malawi. He was co-founder of the Linguistics Association for SADC Universities (LASU) - a forum for sharing and exchanging knowledge and research in linguistics, amongst the staff and students in the ten universities of Africa, south of the Sahara. He was imprisoned for three and a half years by dictator Hastings Kamuzu Banda of Malawi, essentially for his poetry, and now lives in the city of York, England, with his family. Jack has published four books of poetry: *Of Chameleons and Gods*, (H.E.B, 1981), *The Chattering Wagtails of Mikuyu Prison* (H.E.B, 1993), *Skipping Without Ropes* (Bloodaxe Books, 1998) and *The Last of the Sweet Bananas: New & Selected Poems* (Bloodaxe Books, 2004). He has co-edited Oral Poetry *from Africa: an anthology* (Longmans, 1983), *Summer Fires: New Poetry of Modern Africa* (H.E.B, 1983), *The African Writers' Handbook* (African Book Collective, 1999). He has recently edited *Gathering Seaweed: African Prison Writing* (H.E.B, 2002). His prison memoir tentatively titled 'The Whispers We Shared' will appear by 2005. For his academic achievement, contribution to poetry and human rights, Jack is recipient of the 1988 Rotterdam Poetry International Award and the 2002 African Literature Association (USA) Fonlon-Nichols Award. He was poet in residence at The Wordsworth Trust, Dove Cottage, Grasmere, Cumbria and is now a senior lecturer in English at the University of Newcastle upon Tyne where he teaches Memoir Writing and Literature of Incarceration.

NII AYIKWEI PARKES (Co-editor): Nii Ayikwei is a Former Poet-In-Residence at the Poetry Café (England). He is the author of three poetry collections; *eyes of a boy, lips of a man* (1999) and *M is for Madrigal* (2004) and the self-published shorter (2005), which is a vehicle to raise money for the Writers' Fund an initiative to rekindle creative writing in Ghana. Nii co-edited the groundbreaking *Tell Tales Volume I* short story anthology with

Courttia Newland and regularly edits *x* magazine. He has performed all over the world at major art venues and literature festivals and has just completed his first novel, The Cost of Red Eyes, which has been the subject of an international radio documentary. He is currently associate Writer-In-Residence on BBC Radio 3.

KADIJA SESAY (Co-Editor): Kadija Sesay is a literary activist and publisher of *SABLE* LitMag. She has edited various anthologies of prose, fiction drama and literary criticism, including co-editor of *IC3: The Penguin Book of New Black Writing in Britain* with Courttia Newland and recently, the anthology *Write Black, Write British* (Hansib, 2005). She has received several awards for her work in the creative arts and is the General Secretary for African Writers Abroad (PEN) and a George Bell Fellow. She is currently co-editing a short story anthology of New African Voices with novelist, Helon Habila (Picador Africa, 2006) and she has just commissioned poet Kwame Dawes as editor of her first title in the new Inscribe imprint for Peepal Tree Press - 'Red' will be the first anthology of contemporary Black British Poetry for nearly ten years.

THEODORE A. HARRIS (Cover Artist): Theodore A. Harris' art and poetry have been published in various journals, magazines and Anthologies such as: In Defense of Mumia (Writers and Readers 1996), ROLE CALL: A Generational Anthology of Social and Political Black Literature & Art (Third World Press 2002), bum rush the page (Three Rivers Press 2002), All the Days After: Critical Voices in Poetry and Artwork (UpsideDown Culture Collective 2003), Forthcoming in Rebel Voices (Common Courage Press 2005) his manuscript project: OUR FLESH of FLAMES: Captions by Amiri Baraka and Collages by Theodore A. Harris, is seeking a publisher.

African Writers Abroad is a member
centre of International PEN
Patron: Buchi Emecheta
President: Dr. Vincent Magombe
General Secretary: Kadija George

Howl

If this is the curse, then what is the sin?
This is a land, deep red and baked hard by hate.
And though blessings can seem immediate, rude even,
every despair is more existential yet essential here.
Don't blame the bard, don't. The wind is his kin.

Sankara! And another train disappears into night
and shadow. In this afternoon, light –
heavy as ripe fruit. Taste this loam here.
Dark, thick and sweet as any rum cake. But wait.

To say: this way we suffer is harder than. The plight:
like trying to catch the blue heart of a moving flame
as the candle drips wax into a measure even.
Or nothing. Or something. This surely though is grace:
an African child dying, smile stretched thin, even white.

Chris Abani

I Aprenc a Dir Que No

Catalan

I aprenc a dir que No

I aprenc a dir que No
Amollo en la nit
la veu amarga o la veu esperançada

I aprenc a dir que No

Que ja no és temps de plorar
ni de lamentar-se, ni tampoc
de cercar excuses fàcils

I aprenc a dir que No

Montserrat Abello

And I Am Learning to Say No

English

And I am learning to say No

I am learning to say No
I let out in the night
A bitter or a hopeful voice

I am learning to say No

As it is no time to cry
Nor to blame oneself, nor
to search for easy excuses.

And I am learning to say No.

Montserrat Abello

Shoreline of Death
(In memory of Ken Saro Wiwa)

You strip down,
lashed at on a tatty shore.
Death washes your feet,
fish belly up in filmy waves.
Invectives drench
the fabrics of your mind,
you watch wealth raped,
razed and rinsed away.
Your stern words,
splash and hurt,
uncurl and ooze.
You grapple at visions
with men of prejudice
on the edge of darkness.
Elders who wear greed
like a garment,
spread the thighs
of the land and plunge.
They dig graves of posterity
with shelled fingers.
They cuddle you
with promises,
but bring death.
They rip like a fierce tide,
to suck out your resolve,
with bullets and bombs;
you clutch at justice,
fragrant with fortitude.
You spout, jets of verse,
strewn on their mounting madness.
You become a silhouette,
an abandoned tuneless light,
like vestiges of a rainbow,
a gleam of tapestry
at the precipice of dusk

that glints insistent,
engraving the rock of conscience,
until the shackle of inequity
cracks off. Your soul,
hustled out of time,
glides in immortality.

"The struggle continues!"

Peter Kayode Adegbie

Crossfire

the black burka veils
the head of someone's mother
but does not protect her body
or home or country

if we had cared to know her
she might have invited us for
tea and sweets
smiled when we thanked her
her laughter a puff of wind

but instead
she crouches on the
bridge
trapped in the crossfire
of enemy against enemy

although i cannot
see the sheen of her eyes
i feel her terror
her unpreparedness
for this men's war
that leaves women cowering
their feet wading in their tears

Opal Palmer Adisa

Balseros
A Octavio Paz, i.m.

Spanish

Espacio
ancho
azul-negro.
Te abres
para recibirme
"Entro en ti"
¡No me falles!

Yo miro el horizonte
Vamos a llegar
éramos cuatro
somos tres
A uno, por soplón, lo matamos.
Las olas fueron testigo.

El mar se abre y cierra
en vaivenes.
Bajo un sol quemante
mis llagas arden.
¡Cuán grande es mi sed!

Anoche
una ola
tejió su abrazo
y buscó mi cuerpo.
Logré zafarme.

Atado estoy
a esta llanta.
Avanzo
pero el viento
en voz baja
me dice:
Retrocedes

Yemayá
¡Divinidad altiva!
Acúname en tus labios
remolino
en tus labios
espuma.
Yemayá

Alzo la cara.
Tres nubes en el cielo
me dan la noticia favorable:
He llegado.
Por un instante
detenido
siento vergüenza.

Nedda G. de Anhalt

Sea Raftsmen
(To Octavio Paz, i.m.)

English

Vast
blue-black
space
you open
to receive me.
I enter you…
Don't fail me!

I see the horizon
We'll make it
Once four
Now three
One, the informer, we killed.
The waves bore witness.

Rocking,
The sea open and closes.
My sores fester
Under the blazing sun.
So fierce is my thirst!

Last night
A wave
Spun her embrace
And came in search of my body
But I broke free.

Bound to this tire
I float onward,
But the wind
Whispers,
You're falling back.

Yemayá,
Haughty goddess!
Cradle me
In your frothy lips
In your foamy lips
Yemayá

I look up
In the sky three clouds
bear good news:
I have arrived.
For a chilling moment
I feel ashamed

Translated by Judith Infante and Indran Amirthanayagam.

Nedda G. de Anhalt

This is How

At dawn I hold the lamb for him. First lulled
by warmth, I recoil when his knife opens
its throat, when its legs flail, slow, then pulse

against mine. The blood—
sticky on my hands. Bleats turn to moans
turns to silence. This is how

we kill in Zimbabwe. He shows me how
to retract the head, baring
the throat. This is how the Hebrews kill;

first the artery, then the spinal cord.
He tells how the killing was done
to his own, how one day soldiers razed his village,

forced him to watch them bind his sister, his only sister—
lovely as a gazelle, pure as a lamb—
before coming for him. This is how

you make the cut. He spreads his fingers
into a V, easing the knife between, separating
skin from abdomen, foreleg from shoulder, careful

that not one bone be broken. His voice—
serene yet resistant. On him
they cut tendons, then other parts. We are into this now,

slicing and pulling, forearm deep in gore, washing out
intestines before the heat comes. I take the blade
in haste, cut deep into the wrong flesh,

my own blood joining
the other. I press hard until
the bleeding stops, and we work on.

Late morning, when the knives
are cleaned, when the lamb has been
prepared for the feast, he asks

for my hand, works in stinging
ointment, says: This is how
we help the wound to mend.

Fred Bahnson

Rough Poem

I've caught pages kissing
In the embrace of the book
I've seen some sexy looks
On the eyes of statues in conversation

I've seen truth and lies
Shaking hands in elevated tongues
Even between the eye and the lashes
There are frequent rows...
But no matter how rough the poet may be
We don't shoot him with a gun

Ismail Bala

Why Our Lives (The Song of Sisyphus)
(The following is a song from a musicdrama, *The Sisyphus Syndrome* which was performed in NYC at the Schomburg , November '04)

When they kill our leaders, divide
The rest, the world ain't over
It's just a test

We were full of the joy of struggle
When we forced the huge stone up the mountain high
Young people felt immortal
We felt so strong we could never die

But the trick of the world is rhythm
The space between worlds
Like the chasm between Be & At
As old as we are we were halted
Old as we are we went
For that.

But we are a line of infinity
A beat in the heart of eternity
Our faces change like places
Our being transforms like
Time & space

But the Blue Streak of coming
The Black past of our always home
The journey through life's spectrum
Our touching of the coming and the unknown
Speaks to the everness of our being
The neverness of the not,
The world of time without end

You minds and souls of the Wholly World
You presences & images & ultimate matter
Of what is, you are the was, the is, &
The will be.

As you pass sing for us that song
Of ourselves. As you rise & change
With the moon & stars, the sweep
Of where & when

The Hello, that rings through the everywhere
The Hey Now! That robes whatever becomes
The Blueness of coming The Greenness of
Growing, The Red ness of Well.
It's all right, like you still so hip
You go back to the Black, we hear you
We hear ourselves, we is after all
Everything Now & Will be.

Amiri Baraka

We Thought it Was Oil, But it Was Blood

The other day
We danced in the street
Joy in our hearts
We thought we were free
Three young folks fell to our right
Countries more fell to our left
Looking up
Far from the crowd
We behold
Red-hot guns

We thought it was oil
But it was blood

We thought it was oil
But this was blood

Heart jumping
Into our mouths
Floating on
Emotion's dry wells
We leapt in fury
Knowing it wasn't funny
Then we beheld
Bright red pools

We thought it was oil
But it was blood

We thought it was oil
But this was blood

Tears don't flow
When you are scarred
First it was the Ogoni
Today it is Ijaws
Who will be slain this next day?
We see open mouths
But hear no screams
Standing in a pool
Up to our knees

We thought it was oil
But it was blood

We thought it was oil
But this was blood

Dried tear bags
Polluted streams
Things are real
When found in dreams
We see their Shells
Behind military shields
Evil, horrible, gallows called oilrigs
Drilling our souls

We thought it was oil
But it was blood

We thought it was oil
But this was blood

The heavens are open
Above our heads
Toasted dreams in a flared
And scrambled sky
A million black holes
In a burnt up sky
Their pipes may burst
But our dreams won't burst

We thought it was oil
But it was blood

We thought it was oil
But this was blood

This we tell you
They may kill all
But the blood will speak
They may gain all
But the soil will RISE
We may die but stay alive
Placed on the slab
Slaughtered by the day
We are the living
Long sacrificed

We thought it was oil
But it was blood

We thought it was oil
But this was blood

Nnimmo Bassey

A Candle for Ken Saro-Wiwa

How untell the lies / How pray for forgiveness
when the departed made wise / Demand restitution?
Ken Saro-Wiwa 'Songs in a Time of War'

I have it in my conference folder still
pointing its waxy finger of accusation
wrapped in the black 'solidarity' ribbons
we all wore — which soon became our flags of mourning.
But then no one believed that they would do it, really,
it was all show, the huff and bluff and puffery
of soldier boys flexing their rifles, fondling their balls.

And the theatre was so hot, the air-conditioning long gone
and the actors had been held up on the road,
and then eventually the play was just so static, and so long...
And man, I'd come five thousand miles the night before,
I hadn't slept, I had a headache and jet lag...
I felt I had excuse enough to creep out of the show
before the midnight vigil planned for Ken Saro-Wiwa,

the candlelight parade, the songs, the cussing out and cursing,
pretending threats then pleading Human Rights.
And though I know it didn't make one smut of difference —
those bastards had him stitched up long ago —
that if Mandela and Bill Clinton and the Pope
couldn't change their minds then my brief candle
in that crowd would hardly show...

but still it hurts me now to find it here, unlit,
a prayer not sent, unheard by whichsoever god
might just have intervened... But that's just shit,
self-serving guilt and sentiment that Sozaboy
for freedom would have scorned. Let me no lie, you sabe?
It wasn't candles that he needed, or false prayers
but what he's got — our outrage, our compassion, our contempt.

Stewart Brown

Ardent metall - La finestra de la cel•la

Catalan

El metall
de la meva finestra no és fred,
sinó ardent.
Bullen les mans
quan el toquen al sol enfeblits
tots els dits
Des d'avall,
tots nosaltres l'hem observat
dia i nit
pel delit
que comet. Ens separa de l'amor
més pur,
castra el sexe,
dolgut i volgut, i als meus fills
omple els ossos
de negre lluent,
fluid mortal que reclama ma mort
mentre bull
sota el sol
de la meva finestra el metall.

Iolanda Bonet

Burning Metal - My Cell Room

English

The metal frame
Of my window is not cold
But burning hot
Hands boil
When sun-weakened fingers
Touch it
From below
We all have watched it
Night and day
For the crime it commits. It sets us apart
From the purest love
It castrates
The mourned, desired sex,
And it fills my children's bones
With shiny black deadly fluid
That claims my death
While the metal of my window
Boils under the sun.

(English translation by Héctor F. Bonet)
Iolanda Bonet

Puedes Perderlo Todo.

Spanish

Puedes perderlo todo.
El olor de los prados en invierno,
los cuarenta matices del verde,
el sabor del pan,
el perfil de la piel amada,
el chillido gris de la gaviota.
Puedes perderlo todo.
La casa donde naciste,
la tierra que cobijó tus pasos,
la memoria del mar,
hasta el sonido de la lengua de tu madre.
Puedes perderlo todo.
Lo que sabes, lo que crees
saber, la profecía.
Puedes perderlo todo.
Pero si no puedes amar más,
llora, porque te has perdido.

Carmen Borja

You Could Lose Everything.

English

You could lose everything.
The smell of prairies in the wintertime
the forty shades of green
the taste of bread
the profile of the skin of your loved one
the grey screech of the seagull.
You could lose everything.

the land that sheltered your steps,
the memory of the sea
even the sound of your mother's tongue.
You could lose everything.
What you know, what you think
you know, the prophecy.
You could lose everything.
But if you can no longer love,
cry, for you have lost yourself.

(English translation by Ana Osan. Departament of Modern Languages, Indiana University Northwest)

Carmen Borja

David (2)

people love what they need
what they feed

on: the lips. the fat, the loins. the lungs
that cry out for mercy or in greed
the care. the chilldren that depend on us
those who say they love you so so so so so so so
that you believe it

we love life like that. its beauty its
challenges its benefits
its accustom habitat. even unto its dust

so that even when these turn away from us
betray us

even. we hang on to the costume the custom
of the habit. the dress the slack
trousess swinging on its wire hanger
behind the silent door

we don't like to give up even the poor
ghosts of all this green
come brown. come down. the young now nodding anchor
in the derelict

•

love of country is even more difficult
into this mode of unthankfulness. all this waste of agriculture

yam. stringbeam. okro. bonaviste. parsley. caress
of ceressee . is whe the graves are

unspeaking in their dialect
so briefly. so soft wind among the verbs . unlisssenin yr language

•

there is a long pause here. so that the listeners think wonder whether the poem is finish. xcept for this lean still in yr voice. the ridge or rift of the unmark(ed) paragraph. allowing the dream . *slow. still w/the pain in his heart. to walk about the waken room. feel the slow wooden floor under his feet. the grit where the dust is. watch how the furniture comes slowly back into place. restoring time to its spaces and allowing muhammad to remember how. in the ring. they prepared him so carefully to face the victory of his final defeat. light coming in at the windows. smiling now. on his feet. the mask of the gloves glowing again in the place where his face is. as it*

...has always been. from the beginning...

it is only after the period of this pause. long enough for yr eyes to hear every word here
what the last line of the poem is saying...
...that above it all. there is still the sun. signing...

Kamau Brathwaite

Flight

Enter Mrs Esmerelda Tanager
semi-illegal alien- out of Africa, Tanganyika, elsewhere-
her wrap-design a fine bird of paradise,
observed, as if in hides, by green-tinged beams, with x-rays, two-way
mirrors.

Passengers meet and part like globules of mercury.
Tinny announcements bee-buzz in the tannoy:
A butterfly caught is a butterfly lost, thresholds vanish as thresholds are
crossed, neither are for you, neither, you
who are made from cuttle-ink and ether.
Mdme Tanager is crossing hers, sweaty, buoy

-ant, blood jolting to a *Sony-Walkman*'ed Fela Kuti remix
when the *Fetherlite* in her colon
containing -one gram? one ounce?- splits along its seamless seam

as she bursts through Arrivals
un-announced, to face a man with a cardboard sign scrawled ALBION,
the shot bird taking off in fourteen directions at once.

Matthew Caley

Profit and Loss
For Ken Saro-Wiwa

Benevolent Gods, you honeyed tongues!
You give us gifts to pass on to our children:
Good genes, moral convictions, a passion
for the arts and a curiosity about the mysteries
of the planets. In the great depths of oceans
your splendid hands touch us, we watch the
shark's cunning, giant whales breathe fire!

But other Gods, contemptuous of us,
with a knowledge of how spendthrift
we shall become, have given us the lure of gems,
lush perishables of wildlife and forests,
and deltas where the soul drowns in oil:
Curses to men and women who, freelancing
in every known vice, tempted your hands
until you threw them out of paradise!

Syl Cheney-Coker

Grants Pen

Run a session in Grants Pen
I dare you to sit inside the color of dense hope
folded
fruitful into the shy eyes
of a pregnant woman/little girl dancing
slow molasses
in rhythm and sway

movement is necessary for life
here

nothing is promised
on these asphalt banks of police and people at odds
over the square and who is allowed
to set up speakers there

ride a likkle riddim
here
and watch love semaphore
pungent
on the narrow sidewalks: young girls

adjusting the straps of training bras
brazen
the grandparents might say
of the boys whistling alternatives to school uniforms

babies are born here on one of three
gullies
zinc and black skin
mingle to form homes

on top of everything

the bottom feeders and guns live here too
rape is a matter
of fact

here
death is the tight squat
of rooms and failed examinations
community meetings: events to survive
mothers
learn to ache attached
to the last child—wash-belly
banned close to the security of breast

the first can fend for himself

run a session
and they will come

cavorting rain or shine
if there is music
they will come
watch the smiles
the missing teeth
the venom
the velvet
the dark pleading
forgiveness for the poverty

the murder
the memory of the madness
muted

run a session
and watch the collective heart
beat wild undulations of rhythm
rearing a multitude
roaring willful and safe

Staceyann Chin

The Hangings of George and Rufus Hamilton:
In Memory of Ken Saro Wiwa

January 7, 1949

Near midnight, Rufus slammed the hammer
Down, down—bam!—into Burgundy's head—

Like a bullet bashing the skull.
The night heard a man halloo, "Oh!"

George turned around when he heard.
Inside, the cab bled as black as a hearse.

The moon that night: a white man's face.
Winds flickered black, slick, in the pines.

When Georgie sidled down the hill, glidin
Back to the car, Br'er Rudy already had

Burgundy's wallet tugged out his pocket.
His blood hugged Rue's body, snuggled up

His face. Giorgio shoved Burgundy aside,
So he could strip off cash, watch, rosary.

Later, George parked the taxi, a cadaver
Stuffed in the trunk, in Fredericton's snow,

And walked off, whistling, to drink, drink, drink.
Snow cleansed everything, but memory.

The taxicab leaked a smoke-trail of blood.
Just because.

Georgie weren't chilled; he waltzed back where
Rue be guzzlin blackberry wine in brand-new clothes.

Rue didn't feel nothing bad or wrong.
A white man was dead, yes: but they had booze and cash.

Trials & Convictions

Geo: Everyone says
  The noose is soon.

Rue: What they mean is,
  Life's meaning's gone.

Geo: After I die, let my words be rain, grass:
I don't mind, in April, in Three Mile Plains.

Rue: Gravediggers got job security,
But murderers got no reason to be jealous.

Judge: It will be a crisply, British-accented lynching.
    To exterminate two germs.

The hanging? Will be very disgusting.
Of two pterodactyls. Very disgusting.

The Edvard Munch moon screams like Pound
In night's icebox, while Van Gogh stars go mad.

The Hangings

The gallows is carpentered so passionately
Love itself seems engrained in the pine.

The pale, soft, fresh, easily worked pine
Transforms the gallows into a guillotine.

The two hanged, young Negro men, unhinged,
Swing lazily to a bluegrass, Dixieland tune.

A murmur of light, eh?
Then stars expire in dew.

Some repugnant vomit, this turd, the hangman,
After this Sadean idyll, will cultivate peaches.

No light from lilies in this nocturnal sunlight.
10,000 mad dogs cheer and cheer the boys' falls.

The clangor of two hangings—
Those dangling feet, pealing.

George Elliott Clarke

Swallow

She listening to the radio this morning
Slice of news, slice of weather, slice of traffic
Every ten minutes
No music
No garnish.
A quick serving of facts from the frontline.
Swallow   every ten minutes.

Man explode at check-point, three wounded
Bomb mash up truck, three injured, one critical
Is so news sound to her these days
Take it or leave it
No music
None dead this time. She wonder how critical.
Every ten minutes swallow

She think about him, how he end up out there
How he sign up for school and end up in war
Raw
With a fine education
Nuff garnish.
Is a job, Mom. I don 't do no killing. I'm an engineer
And she swallowing every ten minutes.

War like pretty mas on television
Band looking sharp and camera clicking
She silent with shock
She in awe
He have time to serve
and he serving it, inside
He write her from war. What a thing!

And now is Thanksgiving. He coming home.
I miss you, he write her.
He get talkative.
War make the boy eloquent.
I love you, you hear.
Tell Auntie Genevieve fry plantain for me
The boy want to swallow all he could find.

Cook fish, rice and peas
I want bamie, jerk chicken, potato pone
You have ginger beer?
I coming home
I love you, you hear
Still she swallowing every ten minutes
Is Thanksgiving tomorrow

Tonight uniform in her living room
Man mouth open, word jump out
And she don't even bawl
From the time uniform stop to make her acquaintance
She know something critical
Now she calm
And she swallowing every second

She stand aside to let word pass as it jump
And she calm, calm, calm as she watch word run
A bomb in a drain and the truck blow up
Not the same news she did hear?
Was critical. She wonder for him and who else.
And she wonder if she could go to somebody and say
Dry, dry, dry, without swallowing I take you son and I kill him.

Ginger beer ready, chicken done season
She must tell Genevieve not to bother bring plantain
Another serving of news. A bomb. One American dead.
That straight forward.
Iraqis dead, too, but news don't say how many
Some wounded
And she wondering if anybody critical

Merle Collins

What Do They Care

What do they care about ecological devastation
& survival of the Ogoni people
They're just into
smiling, eating, making money,
& fucking up the planet
They are not concerned about the future
because killers have no future
It's about the oil,
the pipeline
& the road to the docks
It's about selling off resources
receiving revenues
having a place in the global glut
& moving greed, mediocrity & stupidity
to a new plateau of power
What do they care about customs or traditions or
cultural invasion
living conditions
& the Ogoni homeland
They don't speak Ogoni
They speak financial profits
that's their language
that's their ideology
& you cannot change the mind & spirit of those who
distort themselves like Sani Abacha & his friends who
all wear the same uniform
buy the same weapons
have the same name of general
& are a part of the same
corporate committee of shit heads
responsible for
the escalation of poverty
& the organization of death squads

What do they care about
melting ice caps
carbon dioxide
land erosion
atmospheric pollution
& industrial waste
They like to instill fear, show dominance
They don't care about the ocean or space
or co-operating with people interested in developing their community
like Ken Saro Wiwa and the other Ogoni 8.
That's why the struggle continues

Jayne Cortez

Inevitable Step

young tiko's dreams
scatter to pieces,
hang from the baobab tree,

a boom of a thousand drums
in the imagined luanda's
stadium where tiko's feet,
swift as birds, chased
a soccer ball of rags

gravel, grass and cloth
burrow in tiko's stump

in the boot of europe,
a church-going father
designs devices in explosive
greens and sands, calls
them butterflies, toys gliding
to the ground in the thousands.
his sister quit valsella last
month and greets him with a banner
at the end of the day

home at night,
in the undermining silence,
missing another goodnight kiss,
the father clings to his child's hand

tiko's femur
will continue the earthbound growth
piercing through flesh and skin,
seeking its sole

Paulo da Costa

History
('...the nightmare from which I am trying to awake.' James Joyce)

Very like me and you in a beastly embrace
Very like politicians talking off the tops of their heads
Very like my mother the dawn swimmer who parts water with her hands and plaits it with her feet
Very like the earth ready to receive me wrapped in nothing more than a cotton sheet
Very like air which turns me inside out and bears my body away in particles
Very like hollow feathers riding air currents
Very like sky writing inside my head
Very like fire to give with one hand and take away with another of its many limbs Shiva octopus trickster spider
Very like Nicholas my three-and-a-half year old to tell me the weather of my insides before I know it
Very like his mother to prepare for a hurricane
Like light to bend in water oh shook pencil or Hopkins's foil
Like the price of milk to mimic the price of the soul
Like two matchstick children to define a lost continent
Like English literature to leave no margin for error
Like the man who walks with two left feet
Like the woman who flies with her hands behind her back
Like the time I inhaled and thought I could fly
Like the other time when I thought nothing and was weightless and nothing thought anything of me
Like the present whose unadulterated flour sifts through my fingers
The past that flea who bites me and expects me to be its host
The future lined up in waves just off shore and yet always on the horizon
A tree drilling downwards and outwards while it spreads a picnic table for a feast
The morning not to warn me to stay in bed
The night that invites me to its club full of ghouls with dry tongues
Love to waltz into my life and teach me all I need to know about dying
Gravity to hold me down buoy me up turn me loose

My secret agent appendix to flare up in me
My mirror never to lie always to tell a tale of at least two Freds
My grandmother to father me my father to murder me and die young and a stranger to me
My uncle the villain whose life was a sentence whose sentence was life
Very my country to pretend not to know me and others like me who do what I do
Very chocolate to thicken my blood
Very skin to cover me with trouble
Very trouble to cover me with skin
For skin and trouble to fight over me
For skin to let more of me out than in
For skeleton to never let me fall to pieces
For bones to work gristle and hoard marrow to crack and rarely break to break and mend with no memory
For my head of less and less hair and more and more skull to show for my fears
Very like a drum to mimic my heart breaking over and over
Very like a road with a fork in it and no knife
Very like a dinner plate to stack up into a planet of such plates
Very like the man who sucks his thumb and wets his bed and holds dominion over millions
Very like God to absent himself herself from all things human
Very like us to build cathedrals for a guest who never shows and lock those cathedral doors against the homeless
Very like the two of us who sleep back to back after a little belly to belly
Very like you to tell me what Nano technology will do to a steak a placemat the sole of a shoe as I lick you
Very like this art that cries out for transparency
Very like this life eager to whistle in a vacuum eager to vacuum while it whistles eager to vacuum a whistle vacuum to eager over

Fred D'Aguiar

Eat

for Ken Saro Wiwa

If you feed me with the thin parchment
of dried pulp, the papyrus of rivers
that still whisper through deserts
greening the edges; if you feed me
the torn sheets, stained in sepia
with the mashed berries of old land;
if you feed me with the bitter taste
of your commanding, my belly
burns with the acid of your ire;
and I bend over the bowl, water
cold from Charleston's dark rivers,
the flame of my stomach burning
into a winter night*if you force
me to feed on the burden of your heart
I will search for the brittle bush
of sin to set it aflame with your truth
but a man must know when night's
reflux, the throat full of consumed
meals in the heat of the spirit
on his head. Lord, Lord, I can't eat
no more of your words. Lord, Lord,
can't eat no more of your words;
people won't listen to what they heard.

Kwame Dawes

Under the Skin

Excellency
I write to appeal against
the fate
of a citizen
of your country
who was arrested
in the early hours
by your secret police
allegedly tortured
and held without trial
for many months
Is now reported dying
in one of your prisons
Location unknown

Excellency
I know you will give this matter
your earnest consideration sometime
between your last
cabinet meeting of the day
and your next square meal

I, after all
write this in my dinner hour
one-handed
Please pardon the crumbs
unavoidable when one sandwiches
these little humanitarian acts
into a busy life

I remain
Excellency

Sincerely
yours...

Daphne de Jong

Brightness

Along the gloss of the coastal shelf
drifts the taste of the ocean breeze,
and a perfume that pours
from trumpets of flowers.
Up there the sky smudges pastel blue,
as the sun's fire flexes
to climb like the flame
of a matchhead held aloft.
All the dancers of the silver meniscus
are streaming and ribboning across
green, glazed transparencies.
Epic fathoms edge their speckled
fingertips into the shallows.
Inside the cloud of the oceanic self,
soaked seeds begin to grow.
A golden comb teases foam against sand,
and the beach is dazzled
to see a sudden clarity begin to burn
through the silken morning,
leaving the world netted in light
that is caught, that is held,
and then drawn tight.

David Eggleton

Baba Wiwa's Trees

Trees grew from his mouth, vital roots
Vein from his heartland, Ogoni
Painting a forest of frank words between his teeth,
onto the pages of his conviction

Mashing on human rights, his tongue pressing
The virgin oil of tradition and love
I would have him as my Baba
To know what a right to protection was

His pipe blowing potbelly rings
Over the swollen pipelines - open orifices, weeping
Black tears into bloated Swiss banks.
Nigeria gives piggyback rides

At the price of a village. Silver red dawn to golden sunset
Crow heads dip and poke for molluscs
The people lament their bravest storyteller
As his pen glides over smoke smeared skies

The rivers shake their heads, for shame
The treetops cradle a father's name.

Zena Edwards

What We Hide, We Can't Hide From

In Saudi Arabia two men murdered another to keep their forbidden love secret. They were sentenced to be stoned to death.
Metro Monday 140305

I see you opening a door to what should have been an empty room
your presence disentangling our bodies into guilty-love.
Your accusing eyes make a pornographic still of our limbs.
Your shocked face sours our bodies sweating sweetness.

Your betraying mouth spews an enzyme to dissolve us.
We both heard/hear the words that if spoken would be shame.
He sees the moment you realised you'd die with our secret.
Your final percussive music has become our only tune.

That tune, those words would wither our fathers' faces,
still our mothers' breath, have our brothers refuse embraces.
Our tainted sisters weep fearing the loss of good marriages
or inlaw's regular reproach. You paid red-shredded long-breath
minutes.

We pay the patter-prayer. of stones, each thrown to cover,
to deny, to unmake what we are; shroud what we were;
their sons, brothers, cousins, neighbours. "Listen my love
they are playing our song." Their shame, like ours, is violent.

Jeanne Ellin

The Soldiers in the Garden
Isla Negra, Chile, September 1973

After the coup,
the soldiers appeared
in Neruda's garden one night,
raising lanterns to interrogate the trees,
cursing at the rocks that tripped them.
From the bedroom window
they could have been
the conquistadores of drowned galleons,
back from the sea to finish
plundering the coast.

The poet was dying;
cancer flashed through his body
and left him rolling in the bed to kill the flames.
Still, when the lieutenant stormed upstairs,
Neruda faced him and said:
There is only one danger for you here: poetry.
The lieutenant brought his helmet to his chest,
apologized to señor Neruda
and squeezed himself back down the stairs.
The lanterns dissolved one by one from the trees.

For thirty years
we have been searching
for another incantation
to make the soldiers
vanish from the garden.

Martin Espada

In The Ear of the Shell (Stanzas 5-8)
To the memory of Ken Saro-Wiwa

> "The struggle of people against power is the struggle of memory against forgetting."
> Milan Kundera

5.

On the fifth attempt it worked.

Daniel
Felix
Nordu
Paul

the Doctor
Saturday
Barribor
John

and Ken.

Bori Camp, Port Harcourt, 10th November.

6.

Absence is a hole made flesh.

A life's man-shape that
swinging
hurts the breeze.

7.

Strange again
how fear remains for power,
how power fears the corpses it has made.
As though the acts it does change nothing for it,
merely white words on the whitest page.

They feared his pipe.
His father could not have it.
Perhaps they thought his voice still lingered there.
They poured fresh acid over all the bodies.
The lips still held the last words that they said.

The graveyard was off-limits
(graves are dangerous);
centres of sedition, rebel cells.

And in Ogoni land
at all the junctions
soldiers set up blocks to hinder choice;
and with "non-lethal"
British-made equipment
kept the grief as quiet as
the grave.

But you are not gone.
There have been sightings.

It is said that with the tightening rope
you escaped out through your teeth
and vanished,
escaped as gas flares
firing through the day.

You lifted like the song-birds do
off the lightning-trees
and now you live abroad
and still are working,
appearing quantum-like in many sites:

In the multiple Nigerias of exile
(shaped like hearts
as wide as the Savannah)
in a million newspapers and TVs
in your last interview
in the shell of the ear
and in the ear of the Shell,
your name in us like a funeral
and its meal,
but still food.

We learn and our throats start to work
in a different way.

8.

Now
Everything has changed
and nothing has.
The wound is still a raw meat
rubbed with salt.
Only now there rise nine reasons more to rise,
to help Achebe's[7] Anthills last the fire.

Not to be the authors of grey silence,
simply finding *hard court* in Port Harcourt
Or *agony* in the sound of Ogoni;

not to let the memory
drift with morning.
These things *are,*
but harder,
hard to find
and make the moment of a new
and thriving language
that might in time
rhyme justice and Nigeria,
find song within Ogoni
and its land.

Gareth Evans

The Truce

Another dawn with black trees
a warlike dawn where negotiations
have broken down
between all parties

Earphones hang from the necks
of exhausted translators

Dawn of silence, but for the
creak of empty escalators

Once words were at home
in this city
mischievous, they rustled
like children's feet on the stairs

They were snapdragons our fingers
rifled in the blue garden

The demagogues have frozen
our words to the walls

Now only the wind moves
in an agony of remembering,

and the flags on the rooftops,
the terrible white flags

Alison Fell

No Further

While I stand naked in the bamboo hut
I am my father. Our freckles fuse,
our noses redden, our hair bleaches to sand.

He is marching in the Arakan, his friends
fall at his feet, they die quietly
Jamchapel (Honeychurch), Windy (Breeze), Oscar (Wild).

At seventy-four my father fights battles in his pyjamas.
He wakes on the floor of his room.
A Lancaster bomber painted on a china plate

climbs the frail wall.
He is marching, the sweat stands on his brow,
his nose glistens. His squadron seeps across

a tea-plantation, one man is invited in to bathe.
My father sits naked in a tin bath.
I ladle water over my shoulders,

come to welcome the knife of water down my back.
The scrubbing brush will not rid my feet of grime,
it lines my toenails like kohl.

Should I wash my hair first or my bucket of clothes?
The tin of water is mine, to dowse my sandals,
to dribble down my legs, to scald away the heat.

Outside, a soldier rests a gun
across his narrow shoulders.
He will patrol the camp tonight.

After nine I will go no further than my hut
with its woven walls and roof of folded leaves.

Chrissie Gittens

Bone Music
—for Ken Saro-Wiwa, executed by the Nigerian government, November 10, 1995

I.

Still, there is music
when a drum is punctured.
Still, a hide is skin, pounded
by sun and salt. The fields do not want
this. The skin does not want *this*.
The dream of oil is to rest in the rock-salt
breasts under the earth.

Let the Ogoni tribe pound bones
together until the sky thunders:
What is the cost of bone music?

The poet would not hang. The rope
refused. The wooden gallows
beneath his feet, said:
I am a tree first.

Nine stars dropped from the sky
like cymbals, like kola in a gourd.
The music rattled, some hollow
organ shook.

The threads of the hood over his mouth
stretched in resistance. This hood, weary
of choking innocent men's words, nightmare
after nightmare, said:
Once I was part of a field.

Crude drums make no music.
The dying gazelle, utterly silenced,
tears its own flank apart. Metal Shell
pipes thrust rapier snouts through earth-skin.

The hide of a drum split
to shreds. To *shreds*, weak
rope, the poet's corded legs
dove mid-air: *still*
there was music. Still

oranges and guavas shrink
into sores. The sun could only
brown the white bellies
of dead fish; the sun could not get
its light under the oil.

Let the Ogoni people have what was
always theirs. Now their fish gulp oil
until the pearl-scaled bodies burst.
Children of Ogoni, the hides of newborn
skin erupt into a Braille of sores. *How*
do you read this?

II.

A soldier from Ogoniland told
the woman to walk into a pond of oil.
The fish were gone, the water
was yellow as pus; the soldier's gun
was exhausted by its own fire.

Do it.

The woman was pregnant, wife
of Owens-Wiwa, sister-in-law to Ken.
You are kin to those troublemakers, the soldier said.
The sun could not get its light under the blood.

Do it.

The soldier dragged her into the pond's
busted lips. He aimed the gun at her
belly. Darkness came down like a hood.

Do it.

Against her cries, the contractions drummed
through her hips like bullets. The woman said
she would drown. Her breaking
water fed the starving pond, rinsed
the soldier's boots.

Rachel Eliza Griffiths

Still Life: Discovering Ice
(for you and I)

Think of broken pieces
That once formed a whole

Think of alleys,
And of dead ends

Uncover the rage within and roar

Think of stifled ambitions
And dreams forever in abeyance

Think of songs muted
And of suns blinded

Think of missions aborted,
Think and rage,
Discover ice and freeze

Think of dinosaurs and dodos
Gone, beyond recall

Think of flowers undiscovered,
Of rage suppressed, unexpressed

Earthquakes, the 'O' in Ozone, oily seas, dead fishes

Think of thunder and storm
Think of inordinate polar nights
Then open your mouth and scream,
Never again talk of a brighter sun.

Helon Habila

Tonight

water will reach
the rim of the glass but will not
allow itself to leave the glass

violence will erupt and horrors
will tie themselves to
every bare tree

tonight we will hear speeches
that tell us to open our legs
to scandal like whores

tonight we will see
tattooed waistlines and kalashnikovs
in the back trunks of cars

paralyzed memories and
revolutions behind
every house door

we will see red landscapes,
stones of light, light feathers swaying
in the nightscape

and wrinkles will multiply
on our faces tonight as each
dead rises from its grave

tonight exiles, immigrants, refugees
will be caught in songbirds,
cracked asphalt will recite old verses

tonight we will listen to the cracks of narratives
the screams of those strangled
by the night at night

we will listen to the longing
of purple evenings
under god's robe

tonight love will be difficult.

Nathalie Handal

A Sonnet for the Confiscator

The house you battered is now standing tall.
The doors all creaked, the windows were dark
when you were here, you thought you left your mark.
But you didn't manage to poison them all-
the pomegranate tree is beyond control.
Where you dumped your waste is a brilliant park
the neighbourhood that feared you, full of spark
full of songs, and rain and the hopes you stole.
I wish you could see all of this one day
I know you would cry, knock on every door
beg forgiveness from the sand of the floor
and would pat the children's head as they play.
People would forgive what you'd done and said
if you came. Shame! you are already dead.

Choman Hardi

The Weapon of Speech
(to Brandye, Brandon, Lil Sonny)

Why are the lives of Black folks
considered cheaper
then the paper food stamps
are printed on

Who bruised Lady Day
hunted everywhere
with the blues skid - marked

Streets burned her eyes
were the tires
a silencer
on the weapon of speech

Why was Malcolm's mouth so dangerous
to America
the world for us
is a Bermuda Triangle of concrete

Why did my grandfather bequeath
to me the rust
from his chains

Who hung the portrait
of a white Jesus on the walls
in the house of my childhood

And why didn't anyone burn it
like a draft card

I think I'll do it

Theodore A. Harris

Mushroom Clouds

One day I hope
Imperialism stitched
Between Red, White, & Blue
Will not cause

Mushroom clouds
Stuffed in the esophagus
Of radiation babies
Whose fathers were murdered
In the name of Democracy

Sucked breath
From innocent people
With automatic weapons of destruction
Because black gold
Determined providence

Made Jesus a martyr
Oppressed   conquered –
Controlled a people
Into believing war
Was the only viable answer

Randall Horton

Photograph of a Man in Baghdad

The father holds his dead son in his arms
while the camera clicks and his grief is able to
cover the whole world and history

the father is holding his dead son
because
an American armed personnel carrier moments earlier
was blown up by a resistance suicide bomber

the father is holding his dead son
because
his son had been running after sweets

the father is holding his murdered son
because
the father has been photographed
holding his dead son
because
the Americans destroyed as much as they liberated
so a new fascist movement challenges for power in Iraq

and I imagine holding my son
bloody and breathless
my precious son
all bloody and breathless
and I cry with the man in the photograph

I cry sorrow and pain
with the father in Baghdad
whose son chased sweets thrown from an armed personnel carrier
sweets for twenty other children whose fathers
now carry dead
fragments with the suicide bomber

I shake with anger
as the father's tears fall onto his son
fall onto me holding my son in my arms
the father's tears fall and I kiss my son and then
let him run out to play while I continue to look at the man in Baghdad
and wonder about the funeral
how he handled that

I watch my son play in the garden
and wonder how the father in Baghdad is managing to go about
his life

then I call to my son
have him come over to me
I hold him and kiss him again
and again

I want to protect him from
the sweets of human madness

Allan Kolski Horwitz

excerpt from *on the death of ken saro-wiwa*
(November 10, 1995)

me

it could be me
dangling on the rope of despair
under military orders.
do you remember our talk
the one without words?
do you remember the day
under the german sky
you asked about prisons?
it could be me,
now, without a shadow,
a voice, a thought.
it could be me:
my mother pleading with the hangman
my children addressing deaf ears
and my voice dead.
it could be me:
a dying voice
a yearning
for a tomorrow that is dead.
may those with memories
kill time by remembering,
only remembering,
the shadow of your presence.

night

night comes
when you cannot hear your own voice.
night comes
when the songs of birds are dead,
when you are dead:
night.

tears

the dead have no tears
the living have other things to think,
and the murderer sighs too,
towards his last
for the journey of despots,
endless,
remembered by the number of graves
along the footpath
of power, and memory.
i will not be remembered with graves
i will not be remembered with sign posts
to a grave;
i will be remembered with words,
and whispers,
silent as the echoes in the hills
calm as the waters of the valleys
deep as the voice of history.

Selected from 'Rainbows in the Dust'
by Chenjerai Hove, Baobab Books, Harare, 1998

Chenjerai Hove

The Agonist
(for Ken Saro-Wiwa & the Ogoni 8)

1. Let Us Pretend We Can Write It

Let us pretend we can write it, using
words that fled with the air from the tightening
noose to maintain their ground, words that floated
belly-up in the creek, their eyes coated

with the ash of the fire beneath. Let us
plait to the hair the maddened mourner plucked
from her head, the word that's cry and loss and curse
and ask forgiveness for those that mocked.

But where is the word and where is the hand
to match the heart that bleeds alone? Don't ask!
Pray only to trace the silence and the scream

and fix to its spot of earth
(which the murderer denies the martyr)
the echo with which our cry hallows their death.

3. Hurry Them Down into the Grave

Hurry him down, hurry them down into the grave,
hurry them down before their bones nail my guilt.
Now my eyes are redder than the blood I have spilled
and my vision no further than my gilded chair
recedes into my head to blaze forth my fear,
hurry him down, hurry them down into the grave.

Hurry! hurry! time marches against me swifter
than the horse. Before their blood cools, warned the witches,
they must be in their grave. Hurry to the grave
to bury the curse and their cause so the burning creek
and swamp may stand still for the drilling rig, its foot
planted in the core of their earth by the ace lifter.

Hurry them down, hurry them down, the witches prescribe
sacrifice. At Ramadan, I will prove my faith
by spurning Allah's grace to slit man and ram. Hurry!
hurry! The world closes around me and I see Ken's
spirit singing, his pipe now a gun pointed at me
and I quail with a terror I cannot describe!

Hurry him down, hurry them down into the grave
time races against me swifter than the horse
and my eyes redder than the blood I have spilled
grow too heavy for my face. Hurry to the grave
before my barrel runs over with the last drop
hurry! hurry! and save me from the brave.

Ogaga Ifowodu

New Word Hawdah

di killahs a Kigale[1]
mus be sanitary workaz
di butchaz a Butare[2]
mus be sanitary workaz
di savajiz a Shatila[3]
mus be sanitary workaz
di beasts a Boznia[4]
mus be sanitary workaz
inna di new word hawdah

like a dutty ole bandige
pan di festahrin face a umanity
di ole hawdah anravel an reveal
ole scar jus a bruk out inna new sore
primeval woun dat time wone heal
an in di hainshent currency of blood
tribal tyrants a seckle de score

di killahs a Kigale
mus be sanitary workaz
di butchaz a Butare
mus be sanitary workaz
di savajiz a Shatila
mus be sanitary workaz
di beasts a Boznia
mus be sanitary workaz
inna di new word hawdah

an is di same ole cain an able sindrome
far more hainshent dan di fall of Rome
but in di new world hawdah a atrocity
is a brand new langwidge a barbarity

mass murdah
narmalize
pogram
rationalize
genocide
sanitize
an di hainshent clan sin
now name etnic clenzin

an soh
di killahs a Kigale
mus be sanitary workaz
di butchaz a Butare
mus be sanitary workaz
di savajiz a Shatila
mus be sanitary workaz
di beasts of Boznia
mus be sanitary workaz
pra-pram-pram
inna di new word hawdah

[1] Region in Rwanda where Hutus carried out genocide against Tutsis
[2] Region in Rwanda where Hutus carried out genocide against Tutsis
[3] Palestinian refugee camp where refugees were butchered by Phalangist Christian militia in Lebanon. The area was under the control of the government of Israel at the time
[4] Part of the former Yugoslavia with a large Muslim population, whose genocide was carried out by Serbia

February 1998
Linton Kwesi Johnson

Sleep Well, Ken

With constipated consciences
And profit-frozen hearts
The ogre-eyed oil giant
Connived with the pit-mouthed dictator
And sent you to an early grave.

They toasted your corpse
Saying 'hooray' to criss-crossing pipes
And crude-oil polluted farmlands
That left numerous Ogoni families vulnerable
To starvation and a cocktail of sicknesses.

Sleep well, Ken
And smile at your killers
For though a few feet underground
The struggle you started continues.

Danson Kahyana

Live 8 2005 Made Simple

My hope is spurred on by a little girl
from Sierra Leone
she stands on a world stage
and proclaims :"Protection for the Children".

My hope is spurred on by her dress
she wears a proud head tie
and kitenge made warm by colours
she is a trophy of African hope.

My dream is made large by a little girl
from Sierra Leone
"The children want a home",
she says.

My tongue is humbled
by a little girl from Sierra Leone.
"The children want fairness",
she states.

This little girl
from Sierra Leone
like butterfly
is a vision lent to dulled eyes.

Susan Kiguli

Alfredo Rodrigues

Alfredo lifted his shirt,
speaking scars and nothing more.

Tonight a copper penny sunset stopped traffic,
dizzy with asphalt and
lies.

Monica Kidd

Father, There Are No More Tigers

How far you are.
You opened your eyes
and Buddha smiled down.
An infant's first glance –
temple in the hills.

Grandmother, eighteen.
Grandfather, soldier.
We're all refugees.

You said the monks hid you,
fed you crushed ginseng,
bellflower root, seaweed.
There was a tiger outside.

Three years you hear
chanting, and the dull knock
of hollow squash drums.

How far you are.
There are no tigers here.
You press pants in a dry cleaner
while listening to Gregorian chants.
It soothes you, you say.

You tell a story:
three mountains in the North
our ancestral burial ground, where
the first king of Chosun lies.
I am a princess, you say.
And I don't believe you.

When we went back,
you took me to the border –
38th parallel: the knife in our hearts.
The officer knew our name,
the mountains in our name.
But we could not pass.

Sitting in traffic, you were silent.
The taxi driver on his cell phone,
he was loud, telling his wife:
We must bomb those North Koreans.

How far you are.
On the plane back to New York,
you looked through the window –
a finger on the glass,
told me you belong somewhere
in the Pacific Ocean where
you might hear a roar in the waves.

Lucia Sehui Kim

The Myth of Displacement

It is not what is lost that hurts the most.
It is the thing that takes its place—
like a glass eye that peers into a room
after the man has drifted,

no longer in his bed but
floating, coated in cloth and wood,
across the shoulders of his fellow neighbours,
down the slope of a half-remembered stoop.

His eyes are clammed, his arms origami
sandwiched in a book, trying to remember what it's like to
tell a story: "It was a clear morning like any other…"
But after that?
He smiles.

If truth be told, this is no time for stories.
The man is no longer willing to change the course of history.
One has to remember the way home now—
only the high-gloss weather resistant signboards can liberate us.
This is the way. This is the way.

Through the shuffling mob, the stasis of the eye,
past the half-remembered well,
faces become a blur, fogged by the heat of so many
disembodied mourners.

His body only too glad to be lowered into darkness.

Just as other eyes were turned away, lest the spray of light
blinded those who did not,
the minds of those who remember
forget just as easily.

Remember: the eye had no choice—
it had to make sure everything was recorded.

The rope is to make sure nothing unravels.

Jerome Kugan

Vinc Del Silenci
per Sayfa i Abok, víctimes indefenses del masclisme

Catalan

vinc del silenci
d'un silenci
de paraules closes

que no franquejaran
el llindar de cap esguard
de cap boca

vinc del silenci
d'un silenci
de paraules negades

que no amassaran
les mans de cap terrissaire
de cap poeta

vinc del silenci
per cridar amb més força
amb veu tenaç d'absència

vinc del silenci
la follia dels homes
m'esborra de la vida

vinc del silenci
sang negra, pedres i sang
pedres m'envolten

vinc del silenci
el cel toca la terra
tot cegat de pedres negres

vinc del silenci
vaig, de cos enterrat
cap a la mort

Yael Langella

I Come from Silence
To Sayfa and Abok, helpless victims of male chauvinism

English

I come from silence
from a silence
of closed words

that will not trespass
the threshold of any sight
of any mouth

I come from silence
from a silence
of denied words

that won't be kneaded
by the hands of any potter
of any poet

I come from silence
to cry with more strength
with a persistent voice of absence

I come from silence
the craziness of men
erases me from life

I come from silence
dried blood, stones and blood
stones shrouding me

I come from silence
the sky reaches the ground
blinded by black stones

I come from silence
and go in my buried body
towards death

Translated into English by Nacho Arteta
Yael Langella

Puberty Steam

they started with frogs

severing the tiny legs with broken glass
their bonded laughter skimmed the lake
ripples forming a headstone for the cat

a drowning exercise in mateship
in unison expelling puberty steam

they pillaged the village

severing tiny legs with single strokes
older now still bonding with memories
of rippled headstones on the lake

in unison still expelling puberty steam
in mateship now as mercenaries

Josef Lesser

A Delta in the Heart
(For Ken Saro Wiwa)

Prologue

Out of the abyss of origins
Gokana came,
melodious on the breath of God;
Ogonis emerged bearing the earth
with its Niger.

They came with the knowledge
that from the beginning
they are one with the earth.
They feel its pain.

Part One

Ancestors parted aeon's curtain mist.
They came with the burden of knowing
fixed on their faces like the chisel's bite
on masks of ancient, African oak.
Forgotten mythologies
lived again on their tongues.

They took Saro Wiwa
by the mind, led him
to a place of benediction.

"The Meiyo is your yoke of pain," they said,
"see visions of strangers come
with no pretence at diplomacy,
driven by the lust
for Ogonis' black oil,
Ogonis' red blood."

Before the Shellmen came,
in days of happy husbandry
when anthills sang of folklore,

Ogonis' life was the Niger
flowering into a delta of waterways,
wetlands nurturing fish and fowl.
Hope was planted
in flesh of alluvial loam,
progeny grew strong in limb and spirit,
firm and wholesome as tubers.
The yam wore a halo;
and dead Ogonis went home to Nature
to keep Doona Kuneke alive.

Is Doona Kuneke dying?
Ake ake pia Ogoni ake!
Odumu writhes, vexed
in his realm of forest undergrowth.
The oil-tarnished bones of birds
testify with silence the cultural degradation.

The tilapia no longer swims
in clear water. Mudskippers choke
on the land's black haemorrhaging.
Owls screech their rage
at eternal flares stealing
the comfort of night's darkness,
and gassing up clouds
for corrosive rain.

Ake ake pia Ogoni ake.
Bring on the priests.
Exhort them to don the power
of the mask. Watch them dance
into that unspeakable place,
return with the eloquence of Gokana,
their healing power of counsel.

Part Two

Too often has freedom
been bought with blood.

I am marked with Ancestors' blessing
for a purpose: a new battle
fought with words; and,
I know my end.

Let us stir up the sediment,
cloud the impunity of status quo,
be directors of our own histories.

Let us take up with zeal
the advocacy of our violated Delta Lands.

With eyes tight-shut I see those visions again
as clear and certain as death:
kleptocrats with dollar-sign physiognomies.
Fear is the energy that drives them.

Somewhere in the infernal recesses
of their being they must smell a burning,
but not of oil. What is the odour
of a soul burning?

Come. Let us,
this multitude with the desire for justice,
in one voice condemn perpetrators of ecocide.
Our Ancestors approve,
our Niger Delta Lands approve.

Epilogue

My life's breath
is shocked into darkness.
The noose exhorts an unfamiliar freedom.
I move now in a country
where the rope and the bullet
are ineffectual; they meet no resistance.

A cause is given the power to survive;
and a regime has committed
a slow, insidious suicide.

John Lyons

Scots

Ye wur an awfu man!
A richt bother, in fact.
Ye an yer gang gaun
stravaigin owre the kintrae,
fechtin the polis.

Aye, I weel mind the nicht
ye got intae a stour
ootside the Cross Keys.
Be richt they sud hae taen ye
then... but they didnae!

Naw... ye ay had the swick
o joukin in an oot,
landin a guid punch
then meltin ghaistlik awa
gin they cud catch ye.

There's bin mony a whap
twix then an noo in touns
up an doon the land,
some lang minded, whiles ithers
are lang syne forgot.

And e'en tho yer body
has lang bin quartered tae
the warld's fowre corners,
ye're aften tae be seen still
fechtin the polis,

in Ogoni, Faslane,
Iraq , Londonderry ,
Tiananmen Square ...
tormentin tyrants a'where
wi yer muckle sword.

Andrew McCallum

Wallace

,

You were an awful man!
A right bother, in fact.
You and your gang
roaming the countryside,
fighting the police.

Yes, I well remember the night
you got into a battle
outside the Cross Keys.*
By right they should have captured you
then... but they didn't!

No... you always had the knack
of dodging in and out,
landing and good punch,
then melting ghostlike away
before they could catch you.

There's been many a blow struck
between then and now in towns
up and down the land,
some memorable, whilst others are long since forgotten.

And even though your body
has long since been quartered to
the world's four corners,
you're often to be seen still
fighting the police,

in Ogoni, Faslane,
Iraq , Londonderry ,
Tiananmen Square ...
tormenting tyrants everywhere
with your great sword.

*Early in his career, Wallace fought a small skirmish against a company of occupying English soldiers at Cadger's Brig, which is adjacent to the Cross Keys Hotel in my hometown of Biggar. The bridge is named in commemoration of this skirmish, 'the Cadger' being one of the clandestine names by which Wallace was known at the time.

Andrew McCallum

From Dublin to Ramallah
for Ghassan Zaqtan

Because they would not let you ford the river Jordan
and travel here to Dublin, I stop this postcard in its tracks –
before it reaches your sealed-up letterbox, before yet another
checkpoint,
before the next interrogation even begins.

And instead of a postcard, I post you a poem of water.
Subterranean subterfuge,
an indolent element that slides across borders,
as boundaries are eroded by the fluency of tongues.

I send you a watery bulletin from the underwater backroom
of Bewleys' Oriental Café,
my hands splintered by stainedglass light as I write,
near windows thickened with rain.

I ship you the smoked astringency of Formosa Lapsang Souchong
and a bun with a tunnel of sweet almond paste
set out on a chipped pink marble-topped table,
from the berth of a high-backed red-plush settle.

I greet you from the ranks of the solitary souls of Dublin,
fetched up over dinner with the paper for company.
Closer to home and to exile,
the waters will rise from their source.

I give you the Liffey in spate.
Drenched, relentless, the soaked November clouds
settle a torrent of raindrops
to fatten the flood.

Puddles pool into lakes, drains burst their sides,
and each granite pavement's slick rivulet has the purpose of gravity.
Wet, we are soaking in order to float.
Dogs in the rain: the cream double-decker buses steam up and stink

of wet coats and wet shopping,
a steep river of buses plying the Liffey;
the big circumnavigations swing in from the suburbs, turn,
cluster in the centre, back off once more.

Closer to home and to exile:
I seek for this greeting the modesty of rainwater,
the wet from ordinary clouds
that darkens the soil, swells reservoirs, curls back

the leaves of open books on a damp day into rows of tsunami,
and, once in a while, calls for a song.
I ask for a liquid dissolution:
let borders dissolve, let words dissolve,

let English absorb the fluency of Arabic, with ease,
let us speak in wet tongues.
Look, the Liffey is full of itself. So I post it
to Ramallah, to meet up with the Jordan,

as the Irish Sea swells into the Mediterranean,
letting the Liffey
dive down beneath bedrock
swelling the limestone aquifer from Hebron to Jenin,

plumping each cool porous cell with good Irish rain.
If you answer the phone, the sea at Killiney
will sound throughout Palestine.
If you put your head out the window (avoiding the snipers, please)

a cloud will rain rain from the Liffey
and drench all Ramallah, drowning the curfew.
Sweet water will spring from your taps for *chai bi nana*
and not be cut off

Ghassan, please blow up that yellow inflatable dinghy stored in your roof,
dust off your compass,
bring all our friends,
and swim through the borders from Ramallah to Dublin.

Sarah Maguire

This is not a Massacre

"What kind of war is this?" Amira Hass, Ha'aretz , April 19, 2002 .

This is a humanitarian operation.
All efforts have been made to protect
civilians. Homes demolished
above the heads of owners
ensure the absence of booby-traps.
Surely the dead are grateful:
this operation saved lives.

Our task is damage control.
Keep out the medical teams.
Let the voices beneath the rubble
fade away. Keep out the Red Cross,
the ambulances, the international observers,
the civilians bearing food and water:
mercy has no place
in the "city of bombers."

Extermination of vipers' nests
requires absolute precision.
Ignore the survivors
searching through ruins for shards
of their lives: a plate, a shoe,
a cup, a sack of rice. Ignore
the strewn body parts,
the leg poking out yards away
from a white and bloated hand;
the boys cradling a small charred foot.
Dismembered bodies
cannot remember themselves.

What remains? Only traces.
That photo (dead girl,
hand clutched at her side,
once-white ribbon still discernible
on her pallid profile,
ashen skin melting into the dust
that clogs her mouth):
nothing more than shadow
of the drowned, odor of mint
wafting from a grave.

Say it fast over and over:
this is not a massacre this
is not a massacre this is not
a massacre this is not a
massacre this is not
a massacre this is not a

massacre

(for the people of Jenin, Palestine)

Lisa Suhair Majaj

Ken Saro-Wiwa's Pipe Still Puffing

Yesterday, I stopped at another
shell petrol station and recalled how
you'd have loved to puff from your pipe
there, for your Ogoni people and land.
I did not, of course, stop to fill up with
petrol, definitely not; I stopped only
to have a good pee, as promised I would
when they got you executed. Today,
I thought, well, why don't we treasure
the moment we once shared?

Jack Mapanje

saro-wiwa!

what color blood do *these* vampires suck
when their appetite causes hysteria
U.S. green   the color of a Shell truck
black like the oil that chokes Nigeria

what kind of blood do *these* vampires rescind
when their white teeth break the necks of writers
hung in pools of blood wounded like the wind
yet never breaks freedom or her fighters

what amount of blood do *these* vampires want
the blind scale of justice minus the truth
land locked in the belly of a gas tank
blood refineries with no other use

corporate power's calculated greed
always taking what the people need

Tony Medina

There are Oceans Left to Kill

Now they are shooting holes in all the holy leaders. But we
don't know who they are. We are trapped between Iraq and
a hard place. A burial ground, a land of insurgents and veils.
Who is shooting whom? Men die and women die and children die
and yesterday someone dropped a dead body from a car and pulled
out a gun and shot the body again and again and it didn't matter if it
was someone who was Shiite, Sunni or Syrian. The blood all flows
together and lately what was a stream is now a river. There are oceans
left to kill. There is blood on the windowsill and blood on the floor.
There is blood knocking on the door and blood dancing barefoot in
the road. There is blood praying at the mosque and blood calling
people to prayer. There is blood saluting the living and blood burying
the dead. There is blood in Baghdad and blood singing in Babylon.
There is blood on a face and blood on a hand. There is blood without
a head and blood on a knife. There is blood on me and there's blood
on you. There's blood on the flag and blood on the books. They are
shooting holes into air and into bones and flesh. They are shooting
into dreams and shooting out nightmares. They are shooting soldiers
and they are shooting fools. They are shooting into schools and
shooting out wombs. They are shooting mothers and cousins,
grandfathers and aunts. They are shooting uncles and brothers, sons
and lovers. They are shooting daughters and sisters and shooting each
other. There is no death left. There are no trees. There is no wind.
There is no breeze. There is just a hole the size of life. A hole the size
of death. There is only one coffin left. Now who will stand in line to
wait to die? Who will wait to be shot? Who will wait to kill? Who will
call the doctor? Who will pay the price? Who will make the sacrifice?
Whom should we forgive? What sinner will confess? Which God made
this mistake? What night now finds its end? What day is this that
breaks? What more can we endure? What bird no longer flies? What
man no longer loves? What silent heart must learn the song of peace
again? And sing again, and dream again, and come again.

E. Ethelbert Miller

Some Seasons

for Ken Saro-Wiwa, on 1st anniversary of his execution

Some seasons are like that,
beginning innocently enough
a muffled sneeze at lunch
tickling at the back of the throat
you try to dismiss with a quick cough
and overnight your body's flung
into a clammy pit, the chattering
of your teeth loud enough to awaken
unquenchable thirst in the old dog
dozing by your bed.

The dog spits blood, malevolent patterns
cris-cross the floor you scrub
hands shaking with premonitions
you can only translate into sighs
your mother stops eating, her bowels
the seat of conflict so bitter
it can hardly be contained
under one roof.

Surely enough, in the civic elections
your vote, as if by magic, is wasted
on all counts, your country once again
contemplates suicide and a disgruntled
citizen of a faraway land
dispatches the prime minister
guilty of courting peace.

The cup not yet full enough, the gut
swollen with need which blindly
presses on to grip the entire globe
a poet hangs by the neck
for turning his words against the hand
that wanted to feed him
his own children.

Anna Mioduchowska

Thank God for Bono, But

before the scales fell
from his baby blues,
there was Ken—indigo
skinned and unsung, breathing
revolution.

Before *Live* this and *Live* that,
Ken had enough
of red rivers, Africans
strewn like locusts
and deltas plundered barren.

Before musicians and actors took
any stage, this Ogoni son
wrote, protested and released his soul
with eight faithful others
above their beloved, plagued
countryside—eschewing
the elder pageantry only Mandela
and a precious few have tasted.

Before it was his turn
to break open and burn
like a fatted calf for the cause,
strife parted for a sacred instant
under his cane of a voice
thundering throughout Port Harcourt
and UN corridors:
We all stand before history.
I and my colleagues are not the only ones on trial.
Allah shall punish the oppressors.
come the day.

Kamilah Aisha Moon

My Son is a Terrorist

My son is a terrorist,
He's disturbing my peace.
My son is a terrorist,
I'm informing the police.

He looks like an Al Qaeda,
His beard needs a trim.
I read a terrorist profile,
It sounded just like him.

He criticises the government,
Shouts at politicians on TV.
Brainwashed by fanatics,
He no longer listens to me.

An ASBO is needed,
Quick, there isn't much time.
Bring in ID cards,
He's already plotting crime.

He called Sir Bob a puppet
Like blasphemy to a saint.
Lennon and McCartney lead us,
It is treason to dissent.

I don't know why he's angry
When poverty's gone for good,
We are addressing climate change
And we're giving Africa food.

My son is a terrorist,
Arrest him, clap him in chains.
He doesn't work alone,
And I can name names.

The ringleader could be Chomsky,
Klein, Curtis, Pilger or Monbiot.
Each one preaches hatred
These instigators need to go.

They publish propaganda,
Distort the truth, tell lies,
A communist organisation
Calling explosion from the skies.

Dropping bombs in a no-fly zone?
An illegal act to provoke?
Not a single word of this
Sir Trevor McDonald spoke.

Millions killed by sanctions?
UN provides excuse for war?
I refuse to listen to lies,
Take this slander from my door.

Please, arrest my son,
Tap phones, spy upon e-mail,
He's embarrassing his mother
He needs to be in jail.

Dangerous, a mind of his own,
He could inspire others to think.
We live near a mosque –
That must surely be a link.

Check his library records,
Take him away, erase his brain,
Return him like he used to be:
Sweet, innocent and sane

Cuba's nice this time of year
Or darkest Uzbekistan,
Somewhere secret off the map
So as not to upset his Gran.

He needs to be re-programmed.
Lock him up, make him see sense.
Install some patriotic values.
Torture him till he repents.

We used to watch Transformers,
Football with Des on Grandstand.
Bring back the boy I love,
He just doesn't understand.

Simon Murray

Famine Injection

is a plan a plan
is a plan yes a plan
destroyin wi lan
wid dem radio active reaction

atmospheric disturbance everywhere
3rd world yu betta beware
radio activity on de lan
killin us by de million
now de weak mus get strong
to de longest livva de earth belong

is a plan a plan
is a plan yes a plan
destroyin wi lan
wid dem radio active reaction

growin food fi sell to dem
wat about our children
industalizin your piece of earth
what dat really worth
dams buil up everywhere
yu nuh si dem nuh care
beware beware

is a plan a plan
is a plan yes a plan
destroyin wi lan
wid dem radio active reaction

divide an rule is de game
act of god dem seh fi blame
but yu nuh si
is only wi
a feel de drought
nuh food a wi mout
wi sell to dem
an buy it back agen

a terrible cycle wi inna mi fren
but call mi mad
is not an act of god

is a plan a plan
is a plan yes a plan
destroyin wi lan
wid dem radio active reaction

star wars is a reality
weather mishaps in de galaxy
temperatures of minus degrees
now everyting mus freeze
food aid is de cry
while they sit an misuse de sky
wakeup now men of high

is a plan a plan
is a plan yes a plan
destroyin wi lan
wid dem radio active reaction

Mutabaruka

Ken Saro-Wiwa: We Remember You

The grieving harmattan winds,
after years of sorrow,
have finally swept away
the last footprints of Ken Saro-Wiwa;
carrying each grain of dust,
containing tiny seeds of freedom,
across the high seas,
and torrid deserts,
to lonely hearts yearning for freedom
from the mountains of Bolivia,
where Indians survive
according to the ways
of their ancestors;
to the forests of the Kongo,
where babies are born on the run
in cycles of wars and counter-wars;
to the lowlands of Mississippi,
where blacks and whites
still eye each other, warily,
like roosters in a cage.

In these lands and more
new Ken Saro-Wiwas are born,
quietly,
like plants in rock cracks,
breathing anew air
that was denied
by the hangman's noose
getting ready to rebel another day.
For the spirit of freedom
is longer than rope
and tougher than steel.

Walusako A. Mwalilino

Annie Mae's Hands

I intend to be one of those raggedy-ass
Indians, she told them, a grizzly bear
mother, a warrior working the combat

zone, savage with a pure heart. It took five to dig
the grave, bury the body, a bullet in the head, hands
missing, shipped somewhere

across the country as evidence. Annie was a threat.
Wilma Blacksmith dropped her shovel, lay in the dirt
to measure: *We might as well learn*

to bury each other. One more silent mouth
scooped out of Wallace Little's ranch. Later, winds—
yellow, black, white and red—howling cold, howling

murder. On the bier, tobacco, moccasins, beaded
clothes for Annie to take beyond. What once grasped
babies' fingers, traced men's bodies, picked berries, held

guns, waved signs in Boston, fell in the dust
on a Pine Ridge battlefield of two. Imagine: the knife,
bite of that winter day, waxy stain of blood, how

he walked away with her hands, unaware
they reach from the other side of silence, then and now,
signing testimony on the walls of the wind.

Lorri Neilsen Glenn

Letter to my Nephew
(for Ken Saro-Wiwa)

The sun is locked in evening, half shadow
half light, hills spread like hunchbacks over
plains, branches bowing to birth of night.
It's an almost endless walk until the earth

opens up to a basin of water. You gasp
even the thin hairs of your forearm breathe,
flowers wild, two graves of man and wife
lying in perfect symmetry, overrun by wild

strawberries. Gently you part the reeds,
water claims the heat from the earth, you
soak your feet, then lie down hands planted
into the moist earth. You glow. Late at night

when you leave, you will fill your pockets
with wet clay. But many years from now,
you will try to find a perfect peace in many
different landscapes, drill water out of memory

to heal wounded limbs of the earth. You
will watch as machines turn your pond
inside out, spit the two graves inside out
in search of sleek wealth. Many years

later, after much blood has been lost and your
pond drained of all life you will wonder, shortly
before you become the earth's martyr, what
is this thing that kills not just life but even death?

Mukoma Wa Ngugi

Voice

At the bottom of the well,
dry since the invasion,
when even the echoes fled,
rage sits in exile.
To fill the well
is no longer enough.
Mute, this rage
demands a torrent,
demands fast, muddy water.
Howl the rapids, rage,
until mud coats our skin
and we spit
silt and bile.

Allene Rasmussen Nicols

Ken

(extract from *Go Tell the Generals* – parts 1 and 2 only)

I

Now when they talk about the Niger Delta
They will know neither sleep nor cover
no longer indifferent to creeks and rivers
the green earth defoliated by gas flares
fishing havens blacked out by murky oil
crops withering in the mush of toxic foil
They will remember the ghost they invited
an angry first son who'd re-invented
patriachates, roping death to his side
in favour of truth that'll outlast every tide

And, they will say death was not his turn
- even gallows failed to obey the hired jobber
who sought a terminal fare to the churn
of freedom soaring above the blubber
of smoke that told the tale of the wronged
they will know neither sleep nor cover
recalling how death itself feared vendetta
too scandalized to take what did not belong,
it sprang from the technology of wrong ;
traps rigged to humour colonists and brigands

Sure, adream or awake, they'll encounter,
the little man who asked, his pipe smoking
only for freedom to be large enough to cover
kinsfolk - not killing four to trap nine
or stoking fires at twins and hunchbacks
for dark loot. Far from sleep or cover
they will remember who made the past pass
his whisper a trumpet, out-thundering
loudspeakers and wardogs lavendering
biocide as the silted fate of the mangroves

Now when they speak of the Niger Delta
they will know neither sleep nor cover
they will meet the spirit of the Ogoni
a whistle locked in trees, rocks and waters
unrolling forests from incarnate agony:
to dress creeks with will that never withers
hope that traverses every dispensation
to arrive, generation after generation
with an acid vow stronger than machine guns
love of hearth tougher than blood oaths

They will know neither sleep nor cover
While the beaten of the creeks bend double
Bearing the weight of elephant and rhino
Who claim right by size and touted presence
From wrong to ever lucrative wrong
They'll hear no voice of conscience but the chink
of coins and slush of paper money
Harem-throbbing with licence while gas flares
warn the beleaguered of the Delta to stand up:
"we cant abandon fights that wont abandon us"

II

No longer imprisoned by the need for voice,
you speak louder than rainstorms;
in waves that brain experience into tablets,
beyond the placebo,
given to us who are mere prisoners of the possible

you've conquered our confluence with laughter,
overtaken ocean and continent
with faith that outlasts even breadth
beyond dissent; outliving spite and blandishment
your truth overturns tables to save the fruits

in and out of season, you remain the chosen
testament that the creeks wont forget;
nor the turbulence of seas deny
heart of leopards and sage-hood , genii-
of-freedom raising inheritance above lament.

you, who no longer raise your voice,
are thundering down the sky,
pressing the most ancient myths to raise
the lore of the just to a new industry of mind
through silicon fare You've proved it!

that poetry works! above the ruse of power,
hate decrees and the hundred and twenty eight ways
to homicide fashioned by mongrels
who tie pythons round the waist of the Delta
to defeat hope and suffocate dreams

you, who no longer raise your voice,
are the clarion to spurn colonists
poachers of the sibling-hood of the creeks
whom your Word outlasts as tablet,
the destination that myths recall .

Odia Ofeimun

Lips

Differ in form not duty; lips.
Speak
Plead
Pray
Curse
Persuade
All perhaps within one breath of space…
Lips.
The power ensuing between these cannot be rivalled
Creature and creator alike
Maker, destroyer-

You laugh, you lie
You kiss, you snarl
Silent when you ought to speak
Prattling otherwise.
You bare the tongue, the teeth, the throat, the greed.
How come you sing?
Then afterwards you spit, you stink, you sneer,
Sometimes you swear…
I have known you lips, to spew forth good and evil.
Have I not seen our politicians?
Have I not heard our leaders?
If all the mockery you have spun were to become as one
Then how great your mockery.
If all the lies
The countless lips of the world have sung
Were to merge as one
How great the condescension of our souls, how great.
But if peradventure truth, truth!

That all the Wiwas who ever lived have muttered
And all the virtuous that were slain proclaimed
Could be somehow,
Recalled
Remembered
Rewarded
Restored...
Then how great, how great,
How profound
The liberation of the world would be-

Ogo Ogbata

Breaking News

I read the obituary
Of a tree, and a toddler-fish

I pen a line in the condolence
Register of a cassava-stick

I attend the lying-in-state
Of a youth's dream; a fisherman's destiny

I've heard of death
By water
And fire
But death by Oil
Is new, fresh, far
From a cliché.

It is night, yet day
A streetlight of flares
In a land where electricity
Is an abomination,

Where streams are caskets
And the air is a floating pool of
Timed death. Where sea-Shells
Sing night and day in crude tongues,
Throats drowned in oil slicks.

I have read of rigged elections
In this land
But this news of Rig-ged Annihilation
Is Breaking News to me...

I lay a wreath
For a village that used to be.

And read the obituary
Of a tree, and a toddler-fish.

Tolu Ogunlesi

Niger-delta Life

Scent of burnt rubber. 80 jeep rims spinning.
Watch the oil-king display his might
To armed thugs marching to do his bidding.
His convoy screeches through the night.

Watch the oil-king display his might.
Grip your turgid kwashiorkor-stricken belly.
As his convoy screeches through the night
Catch a glimpse of luxury, built on your poverty.

Grip your turgid kwashiorkor-stricken belly.
Inhale eau-de-petro-dollar.
Catch a glimpse of luxury, built on your poverty-
Swear to stalk justice, drag her back to these borders.

Inhale eau-de-petro-dollar
As natural gas flares light the night sky.
Swear to stalk justice, drag her back to these borders-
Your life's misery will fly right by.

Natural gas flares light the night sky.
Your river's polluted by a new oil-spill.
Your life's misery will fly right by
If you can revive fish by the force of your will.

Your river polluted by a new oil-spill,
Your land blighted by explosions and flares.
If you can revive fish by the force of your will
You can bring an end to all despair.

Omolola Ijeoma Ogunyemi

A Half-Million Troops
(for Ogoni youths on Ogoni Day, after a solidarity visit to MOSOP in Bori)

I

The levelling hurricane came they stood their ground
not only the iroko and mahogany but also the *iwara*

the crier's anguished call assembled men and women
young and old, their strength gathered into one fist

that stabbed the Shell-shocked air in unison
one fist out of a half-million upraised hands

the dark storm bent them they didn't break
who have Ogoni sap coursing their veins

they stood upright powered from within
they stood their ground and wouldn't flee

a half-million stood bonded in one voice
louder than the state executive's megaphone

even when they groaned they organised
even when they cried in the rain they rallied

they refused to be branded
whose birthmarks attest to royalty

they sneered at tidbits thrown at them
whose resources have always been abundant

they refused to break their bond
to be snakes imperiled by singleness

they saw fire set to consume their forest
but knew the arsonist would not succeed

nobody could drive them out of the land
no force could rob them and have peace

who always knew the secret of salvation
handed down from generations of youths—

amphibian they took to water
when the land was in flames

& when the waters boiled
relocated to land their true home. . .

II

And they came to the gate brandishing green leaves
took positions in front of their parents and siblings

a volunteer corps of brothers and sisters' keepers
a vigilante age-grade guardian of their heritage

and in their austere black attire stood in combat
against the stolen green that camouflaged brigands

in their watchtowers of holes and tall branches
a defence army trained from the womb

one death didn't deter the league of heroes from their posts
every survivor ran to take over the standard and fight on

they wanted to share what gods proffered to them
but not surrender it to cavalries of state looters

they dared the international accomplice
and took the case for justice to their own courts

where double standards tipped the scale—
did they really care about others deprived?

A people raised on love of their own
and resistance of exploitation they fought

to keep the gifts they accepted from above
they exercised their duty to the proud heritage

they love the deep green covering them
and want put out the arsonist's flames

they love their waters and resources
and want no spillage to clog their livelihood

they love the fresh air they breathe free
and want no toxins to pollute their lives

they massed at the frontline of justice
there's no life worth living in injustice

the old at home provided prayers
the siblings sang songs of power

the death of one from enemy fire
couldn't break the unending column

the torture of their captured kinsmen
gingered them up to throw in all they had

the wounds of their shot brothers
raised the blood of heroes to boil

they knew empire builders are always strong
but defenders of homes even stronger

they knew rampaging brigades are senseless
the innocent armed by the will of survival

Ogoni youths died fighting
their dead fought on in death. . .

Tanure Ojaide

Blood for Oil
for Ken Saro-Wiwa and MOSOP*

oil and water do not mix

so when 300,000 Ogoni marched
to protect the marshes
crying *"doonu kunete"* [honor the land]
the Abacha regime replied by denying them their rights
and holding them hostage in their own homes
surrounded by the barbed-wire of pipelines
and patrolled by storm-troopers armed to the teeth by $hell

and then they arrested you

for eight weeks you were locked in a cage
scratching defiance in the dust
while they lied on you
contrived charges
slander campaigns
but your integrity remains
rooted deep as the trees

the criminals are the capitalists
that stole the resources from the land
made knights by British royalty
while your people receive no royalties

in their crusade for crude

disease still seeds the soil
cancer grows like the grass
that once grew along the riverbank

the crickets no longer congregate there
their chorus of kora and gonge sounds
have been silenced by the fumes
that flood the atmosphere

in this war
the bullets are the very bread
the children eat
live in the mouth of death

they stopped your breath
that blessed the air with conviction

you met your fate
choking at the end of rope
while your people
choke from $hell's fumes

the very ground you guarded
forced to swallow your blood
coughed up your spirit to the air
you defended

the river you tried to rescue
received your blood as sacrament
the streams are now your veins
your life lives on in the land

you who loved your artist countrymen
Wole, Chinua and Fela
but who will love you?

the leaves do
as do their trees
and the air you breathed
the water that washed you
whispers your name
in the wind
as prayer
to your people who praise you

but when the lightning strikes
and cracks the sky
in that flash
your face resides
and we hear your spirit cry

Justice!

*MOSOP - Movement for the Survival of the Ogoni People

Ewuare Osayende

The Man Who Asked Tall Questions
(for Ken Saro Wiwa)

To the accompaniment of music: part martial, part threnodic. Heavy drums; occasional flute; ululations, brightening towards the end.

I

The hyena has murdered Thunder's son
An angry fire consumes the land. . .

Uniformed plagues subdue the streets:
Crimson boots, a cartridge of curses;
Viper-belts caress the beasts' their waists
Dreams die in their hands

They launch a thousand guns against the Word
Dump innocent songs in voiceless dungeons
Then proclaim to a wondering world:
"As long as we hold the reins,

All commonsense shall be in exile"

And so their hangmen parade the land,
Broken justice between their grins
The nation's head squats on a crooked neck
To every hamlet its gallows

Creaking chains, medieval edicts,
Wounded dreams limp in sleepless terror
A wilderness of thorns erupts,
Seething serpents on every branch

The hyena has murdered Thunder's son
An angry fire consumes the land

IV

Crimson screams in Agonyland
Crimson screams in Agonyland
Where the Atlantic empties the Niger
Into gunboats and crowded crossings

Crimson screams in Agonyland
The Delta fans out a hand of unequal fingers
Knuckles stiff with centuries of accumulated terror
Crimson screams in Agonyland

Fishes fry in the ocean's belly
Cassava rots in the earth
An endless fire roasts the sky
Oily plagues leave a corpse in every home

Shell-shocked,
Our Delta is battleground of rigs and rows
The goose which lays the golden egg
Lies sick and spent in viscous perversity

Crimson screams in Agonyland
The moon dabs its face with a tattered shawl
Crimson screams in Agonyland
Dawn's door creaks open to wayward winds

V

And a short man was seen asking tall questions,
His pen long as Memory
His ink bluer than the sea.
His songs stitched our tattered sails

He brewed a tempest in the hyena's slumber,
Towncriering a tune so terrifically true
Surprising lucrative perfidies with a mirror
Which insists on naked candor

Oh this darkling plain
Dim again with incestuous slaughter!
When the General's hangmen came at last
They noosed a hurricane and a thousand furies

A murdered peace bleeds
A murdered peace bleeds the land
The mountain counts its rosary of tears
Rivers run red with rage

Martyred dreams dangle in our territory of terror
A martial darkness descends from a the sky
An urgent lightning holds a candle to the gloom:
Come Thunder: exact your wrath

The hyena has murdered Thunder's son
An angry fire consumes the land.

Niyi Osundare

from *The Dangerous Journey*

Quotations from Ken Saro Wiwa, On a Darkling Plain

Migrating herds of zebra, wildebeest and Thompson's gazelle migrate every year from south east Serengeti in Tanzania to Kenya, crossing the Mara river as they go; then re-crossing to get back to the phosphorus in the Serengeti grass

NIGHT

Then spoke the thunder, shattering the looming blackness of our national life. The rumble that breaks a spell of the dry season.

- Saro-Wiwa, "The Storm Breaks"

Does a zebra foal dream? Head lower, lower
under lenticular dark cloud, he drags
harlequin fetlocks, porcelain
quails' egg hooflets through pimpling dust,

now slower, slower through the silver
rainbow night, this soot and fester
cellar-lighting, electricity of the blue and evil eye.
Night ringed with eyes, gutter-glow

of theatre lights from lion, leopard, hyena,
caracal (that caramel cat with the ear tufts,
desperate to feed six cubs).
All watching the lame foal,

weakened by drought. All you know is,
you *don't* know, and are afraid. Moonshadow
where the big rocks laugh apart.
Predator-senses. Cilia. Heat detectors,

crowding this long auditorium
for the midnight shuffle-plains,
radar in on bodies, fluids, flesh-molecules
that do not know they glow, they draw.

Let's give him one dream-memory,
one zebra wish fulfilled in dazing plod:
look boy, a sheer green wall of sugarcane!
And yes, he's made it through

into the bleach, blaze, curdled rose
over indigo and lard, the granult scar
of dawn. One more dawn nearer the water.
Big sky, blood-tufted, blood-hemmed,

rushes over him like the white bowl
at the end of things, the little
safe horizon on a pilot's dial
or an inventory of therapeutic gems.

VULTURE

I do not now remember what I thought of, all that journey, but the danger of what we were doing did not feature much. I willed with all power at my disposal that we should arrive safely at Lagos. Miles and miles of calm waters and mangrove forests, and the little dug-out creeping on slowly, ever so slowly.

Ken Saro-Wiwa, "Dare to Be Free"

Raising chicks in the dry season
over a precipice, father has spread
six foot span of gloss-mantle wingshadow,
leaning his white neck (bare for the maggot-plunge)

over four hot hungry fledglings. Guides flesh-threads
into red maws, checks on the herds
he has followed for weeks, alert
for just these signs of weakening: knee-buckle,

flop-flurry, foal-knuckle, mare's hanging head,
black whiskers puzzling, breath stirring fur
on thin tummy heaving where stripes fade
to cream. Ants cluster on moisture,

eye-membrane and pulsing inner lid.
So… vulture-wing rattle, beak-plunge to tasselled
shreds. Ants between slice-opened muscles.
A foal, a living feast. So the trek exacts its toll.

Ruth Padel

Landowners

What does it mean to own a half-hectare?
I stood on the bank of the stream

and asked the stones and the pools:
how deep do my boundaries extend,

through how many seams of mantle?
How high? Up to where the indigo sky

is feathered with black?
For a full hour the cork oaks were silent

while I questioned each leaf.
Then a voice came from the branch

and I saw two kingfishers.
Tchi chee, they said, *kwee kwee,*

and I knew they were speaking
the lost language of the land,

that this estate I'd inherited
was theirs.

Their costumes confirmed it –
wings of the intensest sun blue

shimmering like atmospheres
over the bronze earths of their bodies.

Pascale Petit

Repossession

All over the green planet oil revokes its loans.

Down the long leg of the catwalker fishnets melt
to mesh-work tobacco spittle. Asphalt picks itself up:
each scaly skin spread between kerbstones is pulling

free with a bass pop – each streetmap a kicked nest
of adders coiling up into a spitting rope of black.
All along their spines household molecules un-

crack – hydrocarbon vertebrae whose Lego atoms
snap back into place in a chiropracty of electron-volts.
Cars at last cough up – judder to a stop – dig ignition-deep

to splutter black apologies across the crisp white shirts
of their hosts. And every sump on every scrap-heap
bumps and boils its box-black kettle – rejoices openly

as through the stratosphere carbon and water-vapour
recombine: weave fine mists of oil to drop black
tapeworms of cirrus. Videos slime in the hand like

jumbo choc-ices. CDs in the rack pucker and shrink
to mushy black peas. Dentures gum up the works
in toothless grins of black surprise. Those precise

blocks and avenues of electronics crinkle up dark
and mediaeval. In the fast lane of the bowling alley
a viscous cannonball splashes ten full bottles of

the devil's milk – while those whose mobiles turned
all the world down to its last nook into Porlock hell
shriek as they peel hot tar from lobes – Yes every

biro mothball racquet sags bleeds gutters
till the black string vest of tributaries untangles –
climbs through the shorn pate of ozone. Finally

we notice. On satellite screens Presidents track
their black candyfloss economies writhing round
the earth's spindle – are caught on camera in black

lipstick leaning to kiss the VDU goodbye – and for
that moment the globe has a single gathering purpose
as a girl glances up from her fractions to witness

the filaments merge in that mother of all twisters.
Merge and rise and take its place. She watches
the whole black mass lift up and out into daytime

where it balls itself – steadies a wobbling edge
against blue to sling there its low fat circle – crude
and glossy. She sees the birth of the full black moon

that lights our ways with dark.

Mario Petrucci

London, 9 June 1940

When I was in the Atlanta Federal Prison,
I chanted through the silence, "Keep cool,
keep cool," for I didn't want to see strange
fruit hanging from the flowering dogwood.
When I emerged from the caverns of Spanish
Town District Prison, the children hurled
stones at my head like I was some lame poet,
Even after my first betrayal, when Amy tumbled
with a Judas, you ignored me, and said I made
us "a laughingstock to the world." But I took it all
because I knew you were blind to your own beauty,
that you could be seduced by weak-kneed hypocrites
who would call me "a half-wit, low-grade
moron." I took it all. But what has me
choking on my words is not the asthma,
the shortness of breath that has slowed
my heart, my body that will be taken
away soon soon by the whirlwind—
what's left me mute is the broken faith
of my brothers and sisters scattered like goats
on soil where my father is buried,
like the cold white pages swirling in the doorway.

Geoffrey Philp

History is on His Side
In memoriam: Ken Saro-Wiwa

'No,' he said, No to oppression, No to injustice,
No to violence. Even as he stood before the guards. The sun
was rising proper in the East, blushing the soil scarlet.

Sozaboy was with soldiers, arguing with the heart
of darkness. We all stand before history, he thought, and
'No,' he murmured through cracked lips. 'No.'

He could not wipe his sweat mimicking sorrow's tears.
His tied hands tried. His crowded heart pounding with the fear
of the unknowable. He mouthed 'No,' just before

their fifth attempt to hang him. Who will claim
the corpse of free speech, but those with a pen
to their name? History is on his side. And ours. Yes.

Stella Pierides

Struggle

Nobody said
this life would
be easy—that it
would take
shooting hot hate
into our blue veins
to smother the
archaic wails
of people
sprinting from
steel gangplanks
to iron waters
to cotton trees

Nobody said
that those cotton trees
would hang us
by our eyeballs,
demanding us to look
at the soul sores
pockmarking
our red, restless rivers

Nobody said
this life would
flow like a red, restless
river, or that that red river
would be an unhurried suicide:
as unhurried as molded syrup
crawling, like a cockroach,
down the face of a
nameless
junkie who gums death
because life has blown
his teeth away

Nobody said
we couldn't smile
anymore; or that
a smile, now, had
to be a wooden mask
forged with the blood
of a face we cracked open,
like a watermelon,
this morning in the mirror

Nobody said a face
like yours is but
a face like mine:
a wrinkled roadmap
slouching toward
a mother, a father,
who have never
hung themselves
with love, who
never pulled their
parents from that
spiritual wreckage
called history, who
never asked the
dead for relief,
and who never, never
pondered why ghosts
who don't smile
wage their civil wars
between our bone
and our flesh

Kevin Powell

Prudhoe Bay

"I tell you, it sucks. It's a freaking waste-
land. Just shitloads of birds we're not allowed
to shoot. Food's okay and there's a work-out
room, but it's still a real bitch being based
here." "It's awesome. I was, like - wow - amazed
when I first saw that giant pipeline. Proud
too - these fields are the world's cleanest, no doubt
about it, Jesus our Lord God be praised."
Two thousand men work here and hundreds more
come to leer at all the rigs, airports, drills,
roads, wells, waste pits and power plants which gore
the tundra, licking their lips as black blood spills.
The boss, it's clear, has big tumescent plans
to pump it dead with his plump, slickered hands.

Susan Richardson

Nine

Nine men dead this morning,
Torn between the sky and the relentless soil.

I did not turn my head against the anonymising hood
Among the grey stone cliffs of Edinburgh today.
I did not see above me the V of geese departing,
And for the last time imagine their return.

Nor has it been my lot to meet with friends in stealth,
Or gather in the open with them and with a pounding heart.
I have not hidden beneath my coat any unforgiving book
That might betray me with its honesty.

How would I go to your nine deaths, how would I go there?
Brave like the brave of the muddied fields of Europe
Where old men crawl again, this and each November?
Strong like the strength of African song? I think not.

The bowels of my intellect have not been tested.
I did not go to your deaths, taut and fearful
In the hot dark sun. I did not go, not even
With a bellyful of water and my knees like lead.

Did you go bruised and roaring in the raging storm?
Was your struggle fierce against the shameful, bitter faces,
Or were you silent in the face of stone? Your thunderous
Silence that rolls now round the world they struck you from.

Tonight in an old quiet room I listened to a man
Who played on lute, on mandour and guitar
The music of my country's centuries: *Adew Dundee,*
Flowers o' the Forest, Lochaber No More.

His hand from the unknown hand of ancient manuscripts
Picked, held, gave again. In the tiny silences behind
The grace-notes there came a heavy distant sound -
Wings beating maybe, or the closing of your eyes.

Now, ministers of greed and arrogance, citizens
Of facts and law, tell me now that words are for the weak,
Poetry for the slight and other-worldly: tell me
What will survive you when *you* are back to dust.

Men dance on air when they are dead,
So if you cannot raise then hang your heads
And see the rainbows in the sludge
If you are blind to rivers shining in the sky.

Nine dead men between the earth and sun
This morning are the horror that upholds your lie.

(i.m. Ken Saro-Wiwa, Barinem Kiobel, Saturday Dobee, Paul Levura, Nordu Eawo, Felix Nuate, Daniel Gbokoo, John Kpuinen, Baribor Bera, 10 November 1995)

James Robertson

The Oracle of Easter Monday

Listen to the oracle, Kuru, listen, where there is no sound!
Though we never met, my friend, yet perhaps
Through the sorceress's gin charms
In the song of the weaver-bird
One day, we shall meet
But now is the night of fire - listen!

Beyond the cliff's ninth edge, by the smile of the big, black river
They tossed you into a lizard's grave,
To lie beneath the hooves of goat and antelope, the sting of alligator peppercorns
For a thousand years the stars will fall into your tomb of concrete and lime
How dare they? They, who raped their mothers
And gave their souls, all seven, to darkness
They have many names, a hundred, turning heads
Like chameleons, they change their skins,
Black, white, green, blue, yellow
But their names, deeds, thoughts all
Rhyme only with Hell

Listen to the oracle, Kuru, listen, where there is no sound!
On the day before the end of time
When the yams will sprout seven leaves
And the harvest will yield only yoori
The lizards, grown fat, will slip from their holes
And will dance at midnight around the iroko tree
And will speak through their noses:

We will sear the land black like the tortoise-back

We will burn eyes into bone, one-by-one,

We will take over your homes!

Listen, then, to the oracle, Kuru, listen, where there is no sound!

Hear the whisper of the mangrove swamp
Stand steady amidst the last field of ripening plantain
At the river's mouth, cup in your palms
The blood of the rocks, the bones of wafered creatures
Cast back your singing head and drink full of the Black King's breath
Mix cassava with crayfish and peppercorns
Mould the paste of the pear tree into the form of a human being
Feed her light and set her dancing like the First One, the Queen of the
Moon

And in her dance the fish will rise from the rivers,

Imo, Orashi, Dijla

And will drink kegs of palm wine

And with red mouths shall they sing!

Listen to the oracle, Kuru, listen, where there is no sound!
One day, my friend, we will meet
And together, our bodies glistening with raw cocoyam,
We will brush the lands between the rivers
Free of bush rats and lizards
And we will make the music of drum, horn and gere-gere
And day and night we shall sip wine from raffia palm
Until from the land shall rise magical trees, dragonflies, a thousand
golden insects
And the tassles of the maize cobs will dance with a joy that flies
higher and higher
Even unto the streams of the moon

Listen to the oracle, Kuru, listen, where there is no sound!
Deezian, Deebom, Deemura, Deekor, Deesan,
On that dawn, my friend Kuru, at second cockcrow
Your spirit shall rise from your people, no tomb shall hold them
And all the lizards will lower their brows in humility, in respect
For the children, the land, the dreams
They will heave great bags of cowrie
And will prostrate themselves before the black river
In their broken shells they will cower
On that day, my friend,
The people of fish, farm and forest, of port, village, metropolis
From Fallujah to Harcourt, from Wounded Knee to Chiapas Mountain
Will rejoice and breathe again,
In Khana, Gokana, Eleme, in all tongues
And their songs shall fill the sky!

Listen to the oracle, Kuru, listen, where there is no sound!
From the shell of your death, arise, O murdered Wise One
Lift your arms above your head, stretch your fingers beyond the bone
Rise up into the river of rivers, the sky's burning mantle,
Tear your face into the skin of a crazy man
Ascend, dear friend, ascend…
Your spirit is our spirit, the ink of our pens flows from your dreams
Take us high into the river of light! Let us see!
Then, at last, through the pebbles of your stories
Like the stars, like the moon, like the living dust

We all will be free

Suhayl Saadi

Can We?
(For Ken Sara Wiwa)

1.
suppose
the thot
    /police
took our words

seriously

treated us like the real po-po:

cut us down
on suspicion
of being

dangerous, just in case
we actually

are serious

2.
some of us forget
ken's killers
were the folk
who threw fela's mother
out the window

3.
a little while ago
i took a hot shower

was ken able to wash
before the hanging?

4.
everybody be talking abt
the morning after

what abt
the night before

any thots
on that?

5.
when i look into the mirror
of my life
experiences

do i see anything
that would lead me to believe

that i would be willing
to die for my beliefs?

6.
suppose
you had to take full
responsibility
for every word
you uttered
no matter how little
you meant it

"really, i was just joking around
i didn't mean to tell the truth"

7.
can we
afford

not to be
serious?

can we?

can we be

like ken
saro wiwa was

strong
straight up

'til
the end?

Kalamu ya Salaam

like the Venus de Milo,
are much more beautiful without their feet
but if your gaze soars upwards
how not too upward? How?

The Buddhas of Bamiyan
cannot compete with an authentic God,
should never bear the face of even the false God.
You, who are as arrogant as the usual man,
may love more deeply the pity of a headless,

footless Buddha of Bamiyan – even doubly so.
You, who can meditate only bodily,
don't deserve the pelvis of Buddha.
God is the greatest practitioner of art
and her favourite sculpture is a modest man.

Like the Venus de Milo
(if you are the man who dwells on her),
the twin Buddhas of Bamiyan,
armless, can still embrace Afghanistan unbroken,
embrace those who would rather die than keep

each Buddha from divinity: its vanishing trick.
You who have a mind to, who can think as loftily
as the Buddhas of Bamiyan, can miss them but let them go.
Imagine all the fragments whole again,
and our signature on the empty sky.

Eva Salzman

Peace
(a poem for Maxine Greene)

1. Peace. What is it?
Is it an animal A bird? A plane?
A mineral? A color? A drumbeat?
(doowop doowop doo doo dee doo doo dee)

2. Is it a verb? A noun? An adjective?
A prophet with no pockets?
Circling our paragraphed lives?
(dwoodop bopbop dwowaaa doo bop bop doo bop bop bop)

3. DuBois said: The cause of war
is the preparation of war.
DuBois said: The cause of war
is the preparation of war.
I say the cause of peace
must be the preparation of peace.
I say the cause of peace
must be the preparation of peace.
(Blaablablabaaaa blue blueeblay blueeblay)

4. Shall I prepare a table of peace
before you in the presence of mine enemies?
Shall I prepare a table of peace
will you know how to eat at this table?
(skee dee dee dah dah doo dah bop dah bop bop dah boo)

5. Where are the forks of peace?
Where are the knives of peace?
Where are the spoons of peace?
Where are the eyes of peace?
Where are the hands of peace?
Where are the tongues of peace?
Where are the children of peace?
(Peace, Peace, ting ting tee tee peeeeace ting ting tee)

6. Is peace an action? A way of life?
   Is it a tension in our earth body?
   Is peace you and I seeing beyond
   bombs and babies roasting on a country road?
   (bop bop bop bop bop bop bop bop bopoooooooueeeeeee)

7. Peace must not be still we have to
   take it on the road, marching against
   pentagon doors lurking in obscenity.
   Peace must not find us on our knees
   while a country holds hostage
   the hearts and penises of the workers.
   (bleep bleep bleep blueee bleep bleep blueee doo da boom doo da boom)

8. Can you say peace? Can you resurrect peace?
   Can you house the language of peace?
   Can you write a sermon of peace?
   Can you populate the chords of peace?
   (dee dee dadum peace la la la la dum peace)

9. A long time ago someone said: I think therefore I am
   A long time ago someone said: I think therefore I am
   Now we say preemptive strikes therefore we are
   Now we say preemptive strikes therefore we are.
   (boom boom boom ay ay ay ay ay boom ay boom ay ayaay)

10. Can you rise up at the sound of peace?
   Can you make peace lighter than air?
   Can you make peace sing like butterflies?
   Until peace becomes the noise of the planet
   Until peace becomes the noise of the planet
   (PeaceeEeeeeEeeeeEeeeEeeeeEeeEeeEeeeEE)

11. I know as MLK knew that the universe
is curved ultimately toward justice and peace.
I know as MLK knew that the universe
is curved ultimately toward justice and peace.
for "war is the sanction of failure"
for "war is the sanction of failure"
(dobam doom-doooobam dooooood doooom)

12. Martin said a riot is the language of the unheard
and I say a terrorist's bomb is the language of the unheard
how to make the unheard heard?
without blowing themselves and the world up?
how to make the unheard heard?
without blowing themselves and the world up?
(BOOOM BOOM BOOM BOOOMM BOOOOMMM)

13. Most Def said: Speech is my hammer
bang my world into shape
now let it fall.
I say peace is my hammer
bang my world into peace
and let it fall on the eyes of children.
(frere Jacques dooodoodoo frere Jacques dooooo doooo
dormez-vous vous vous vous ding dong ding ding dong ding)

14. Where are the forks of peace?
Where are the knives of peace?
Where are the spoons of peace?
Where are the eyes of peace?
Where are the hands of peace?
Where are the tongues of peace?
Where are the children of peace?

15. Where are you—you—youuuuuuu (click)
where are you you you you youuuu (click)
you you where are you you
where you where are youuu (click)
click—click—you—youuu (click)

Sonia Sanchez

Queen of Ol'Wharf
(for Granny Adama)

From her chair that rocks
on the verandah, she surveys her empire.
From her chair she rocks
squelches tidbits of rice and fish
into a ball in her right palm
rolls it to the tip of her two fingers and broad thumb
flattened by years of threading hair
pushes it onto the waiting tongues of her army of toddlers.
Once she is sure that all are fed
and they have run to play in dirt and sun,
she rinses her hands, prays, naps
wakes the next day to the sound of peace, to the gentle lapping of life
waiting for the envelope her son must bring
every month from her daughter in London, England
to keep her in the lasting days of her reign,
to keep her in rice and pe-pe fish balls.

Yet this son of her land arrives with no
blue-inked white-envelope
but with black gun, peppering bullets
into four year old with hand in her soft puppy fat
innocent to soft wrinkled wisdom.
Granma can't hold off boys who come with sticks and stones
instead of home made nets and fish hooks
curved from stolen spokes from abandoned bicycles.

Boys the same height and bone
as her soldiers who run from the waterside
boys who run fast to keep Grandma Waf safe
who run from where they swim and catch fish on her land
they season, grill
suck out crustations of fish heads,
where fighting is over delicacy of fish y-eye
and peace is made laughing in between picking fish from teeth
with finger nail sideways before juicing out
the taste of fish between same finger and nail -

they stopped shot in their tracks.

Kadija Sesay

Your Blues Ain't Like Mine
Baghdad, March 2003

i was born to a serenade of bullets
to the rage of hand grenades and
the mushroom cloud of freedom's dust

born to the dance of bonfires set in hollow graves
born into killing fields
beneath a rainfall of arms and limbs,
slithers of skin and shards of bone
carried on the wind like confetti

papa waited long
stroked mama's head with oil until the bugles sounded
someone said freedom was coming
and papa ran to see

freedom was the new child
in one long heave I arrived, eyes wide open to liberation
my uncle went in search of water
but returned with my father's head in his arms
and scarlet stained shoes about his feet

later, someone found a leg
and an arm beneath the bridge
soon, the whole country was on fire

your blues just ain't like mine

I was born with the watermark of revolution
born with the birthmark of liberation
born into revolution
born into revolution
born
into
revolution
REVOLUTION!

your blues just ain't like mine.

Angel V. Shannon

Content Metamorphosis

Lord Vishnu's perfumed
body is beheaded in a ritual.
A promise punctured
as a vicious camera's dizzy eye
zooms, splashing mercury
over the face of a city
where I spend sleepless, anguished nights.
A metaphor I failed to pick up
and gleam in a dream last night
castrates the day. The face
of an ageing mother trapped
in a circle of daggers becomes a dandelion.
Exultant, I swirl and leap
into the blue gorge of glowing gods
where a bejeweled Indra of
large-limbed dazzling nymphs
is ready to pounce upon
the innocence of a virgin goddess
stretched on a mossy rock…
One of the nymphs kisses,
holding my tongue and yanks it out, bleeding…
Saliva of my words
tricking down my huge, hairy-chest.
I am left helpless to look
at the shame of the greasy
chapters of a CD on Kama Sutra
while before my eyes,
the virgin goddess is brutally
raped, then bathed,
perfumed and costumed to pose
as Miss Universe before
a tongueless audience to promote
an empire of multinational eunuchs.

Yuyutsu R.D. Sharma

Song of the Confined
(for Ogaga Ifowodo, Akin Adesokan and Kunle Ajibade)

I
Is the ballad of rusty hinges
Chorusing at the corridor mouths
A love song?

The tune reminds me
Of a freedom I once dreamt up.
But it's hard to escape
To that psalmist's place
When the wardens
Keep disrupting my falsetto
when they throw the metal doors
This way and that.

II
Feed me some more
Of that seedy grass
That sends me two octaves higher
And eases the pain
in the days that swallow the weeks
And soar into months.

III
My claustrophobic limbs
Scat in jazzy harmony.
I sweeten the melody
With tired sighs
And dreams I'm drawing
In musical bars
On these deaf prison walls.

Lola Shoneyin

Impossible Thoughts
For Kenneth Bigley and Margaret Hassan

All I have to offer is an end.
It is almost impossible to lift
the knife and the gun. The mass of them
increased, my arm sockets strain white
trying to lift them. I know this moment
before you do. I read the news and become
your captor. Some things are worse than death.

The round almost green nub of the barrel,
it is almost the same as when a wife
tells her husband she is leaving, it makes
the balls tighten into their cavity,
pulls the rope of stomach muscle back towards
the spine. The revolver handle, the knife handle,
those lovely iron-grey rivets, solid supports
for hands with impossible jobs to do.
The machete edge is an innocent time
demanding to be held.

I will hold your hair; pull your head back,
cut you deep as your face closes in "NO."
Jugular to jugular, to save you, or

I will stand behind you, put two shots
right through your head. A small hole where
the bullet enters, the exit taking away your face.
I will take you away to save you from waiting.
To end the hours of your families prayers.
Save you from being the subject of negotiations,
a political lever, a sacrifice, a 24-hour
rolling news headline. Your beautiful blood
painting the cement dust is an end at least.
I will do you this favour to finish
the metal-tongued taste of waiting.

John Siddique

The Man in the Hospital

At the hospital, a man walks the corridors
In his nightclothes through the deadly nightshade.
I have watched him from my bed the past five months
And pretended to be asleep. Sleep is where I pretend
That morning will come.

I have come to know the sandpaper sound
Of his dragging dragging feet.
I have come to know the sound of his mumbling
His stumbling words spoken as he steps
through the strips of moonlight, broken.

I am tired. So tired. So. Tired.
My bed is covered with fresh grass and night sweat
My dog, a red setter, gently steps through the ward door
She pitter patters her way past the other beds
Hunches her shoulders and dives upwards onto mine.
She stretches by my feet.

I am surrounded by breathing it is the sound of the sea
the rag and bone man cometh. The ward doors swing open.
I raise my eyelid slightly. It takes tremendous effort.
The effort of the Egyptians pulling stones to the pyramid
at sunrise. I raise my eyes

He is here. Staring straight ahead. Straight. A head. Staring.
"There is no illness, there is no illness' He rasps
"There is no such illness".

I am too tired to argue. The others too, too tired to argue
He has walked through the shadow of the valley of our breath
Through the incoming outgoing air of the dying
I hear the tears in his lies and the lies in his tears;
Through the fear in his eyes through the eye of his fears
"There is no illness. There is no illness" he says.

Lemn Sissay

Speech Writer

When the Cattlemen's Party of Sierra Leone won the election, the only thing they inherited in the devastated Parliament building was Tito, the President's speech writer. They wished they could hang him, along with the old President, except that he was the only person able to extract sweet nectar from poisoned words.

They inherited him, to put it simply, in the same manner they inherited the empty state coffers.

He liked money and his body was bent in such a way that it looked like he was crawling instead of walking. He had already written a speech for the new President in which the old government was accused of burning fields of grass.

As the new President read his speech to the suspicious cattlemen, Tito was the first one to applaud him

The next year, when the Party of Foresters took over the State palace, Tito had in his hand a speech written for the new President in which the former government was accused of setting forests on fire and causing Great Famine. And guess who was the first to get up and applaud at the end of the speech? Tito was also the first to rejoice at the hanging of the old President.

The same happened when later on the Army of Poor Farmers entered the Palace, knowing that the only way out was with a rope around one's neck. The new President, who was literate enough to read only beer labels, didn't hide his pleasure in addressing the drunken crowd. And nobody noticed that he was just repeating words that Tito was feeding him as he hid behind the curtain. He didn't doubt for even one moment that the speechwriter would be he first one to applaud him when he announced the hanging of the old President.

Who knows how long Tito have lasted if the Students' Party had not taken over the Palace. Instead of bearing rifles, they came armed only with pencils, and without a need to follow the old tradition of hanging. That was the first time that Tito sat in the audience without applauding. His hands were crumpling newly written speeches that nobody paid attention to. Later even his old allies, cleaning ladies, cooks and flag designers, stopped caring for his complaints, and one day he opened the back door of the Palace and left.

They were watching him from the windows as he skipped over the graves of former presidents, then over the decaying cows and the fields of hunger, and then vanished towards the burnt forest.

"Why is he applauding to himself?" thought the cleaning lady.
"And why does he have a rope around his neck?" thought the new President.

Goran Simic

Tide

(for Ken Saro-Wiwa)

Look, look my friend, over there
how those white sand beaches are
turned by the lap of the tide
into wet Black gold by night.

See, my friend, nearer here,
how those flock of gulls,
grow fat off of Black gold;
gulp the lives out of smaller shells.

One day, we will not be here to witness this;
the lap of that tide will make
each one of us a tenant of its waves.

And only the rocks will testify
to the cackle, overhead, of those
same gulls. Each one, spreading
the long lies of its wings,
writing history out
across the thin blue sky.

Rommi Smith

Lament (& Promise) for Ken Saro-Wiwa

When you lived, I knew your warrior's tread,
among others, and your reverent hand wielding
its pen, as it often touched me with its warmth.
And I felt your tears—the sudden rainfall
that bathed you before you took those final steps
through their gauntlet of lies, your measured steps
caressing me, even so, with love.

Now, as then, our enemies plunder me!
Even as they turn my body into a tomb
they suckle at a teat not meant for them,
tearing at me with greedy nails and small, mean teeth.
Yet they cannot reach the heart, beloved,
latticed as it is with the bones of my protectors,
all your bones…

Now, your strident cries echo in the soil,
amplified through me. Your voice prowls
my belly, pours out of my every pore,
lashing the land, stirring the waters.
It breathes in the ears of the young Ogoni
who choke on the stench of industry, stumble
over the withered crops of my aborted harvests,
and who take up your call, feeding it
to the children: *Fight fearlessly…*
History is on our side.

Even a faceless grave still speaks, still acts.
One day our enemies will come to draw more
of my black blood and will hear
only curses reverberating in the hollows.
Though they have spilled your blood,
I do not accept the libation. They will find me
thirsting, unyielding, and unforgiving.

Sharan Strange

Your Gift

A poem for Ken Saro Wiwa

You left
Taken away by those Monsters
Taken away in that horrific manner
Bringing shame on our humanity
You left
When we thought you would still be around
Your courage seizing the future
Your fight showing us resistance

They killed hope when they took your life
They killed our illusions
They killed our sense of being

Why, in spite of everything
Of voices demanding your release,
Asking for mercy, pleading to save your existence
Voices that came from home and from far away
To declare that you should stay with us
They, those Monsters, closed their ears
Dismissed our outrage and protest,
Sharpened their venom
And took your life away in that most horrific manner
Bringing shame on our humanity?

Where were the Powerful
Those who could have put an end to the infamy?
Where were the Oil masters
Whose black gold sparked off greed and violence?
Why did they not stop it?

And now we are like orphans,
Battered and slapped by the harsh reality
Of oppression

They wouldn't let go of you
For fear of what you represented
Of what you meant to the Ogoni people
To your people
And to us all as well
They wouldn't let go of you
For fear your fire would spread throughout the land
And burn to ashes their devilish plans

They took your life away in that most horrific manner
Bringing shame on our humanity

Today we call on you
Let your spirit linger among us
Let it spur us to resist against
The intolerable
Against the unacceptable
Against the unthinkable
Let your spirit visit us
So we never forget what it means
To live and die for one's belief

Let your spirit embrace the land
Plant the seeds of renewal
Let your spirit rise, let it soar high
Let it dance, let it rejoice
Today, we have come to celebrate
A life well spent
Full to the brim

Veronique Tadjo

I've Buried Ten Children

(Ten) Ten of my children miscarried and died between 1984 and 2002.
I buried four on the three-acre farm between 1997 and 2002.
Two of my children, born alive, watched me. All the others were flushed
Down a toilet out of ignorance, the rest destroyed at hospitals as medical waste.
I dug the graves, placed the small cloth wrapped bundles of flesh
into the cavity of earth, moved the soil on top of the remains
as I spoke prayers to a sky that neither flinched nor quaked,
though I expected some rumbling, some pile up of thunderheads,
something huge to heave and shudder at me, this carnage
and the methodical skill in which I carried out the task.

(Little Indians) In 2002, I buried two with my husband Erik, who I married
the same year. We named them, because a medicine woman from the rez
told me that I should name them. So they
would "know who they are on the other side." I named
all my previous dead children 'Angelitos', an Indian
tradition in the borderlands. The first of my husband's children
we named Soledad. The second, Artful Ray of Hope.

(Ten) He had some manzanita wood he'd saved from a date up Mt. Lemon's hillsides.
He shaped the branch limbs into a grave marker for our second child.
The date was like this: We hiked back in the crisp, dry trails,
a scent of recent fires nearby.
His sculptor instincts rising
when he touched a fallen limb or trunk.
We made love in the open air, under an old oak.
The air was cool, and the waxing moon hung above us, quivering.
We drifted to sleep, lulled by the soft safety in each other's arms
against the walls of the world. We conceived.
On the morning of the burial, he carved a talisman,
shaped like a river. He placed his tools, tobacco, and cedar into the earth
with our child.

(Little Indians) I'm showing this dance of hands, needle and thread to
my daughter Maura, five years old. She wants to sew. I prepare
Maura's thread and needle for her.

(Ten) Since I was nineteen, I'd had numerous unexplainable
miscarriages,
one after another after another; torrential storms in the monsoon
season.
One of these stabbed pains throughout my body; a subsequent
depression
I couldn't shake loose. I was in my early twenties and in a marriage
weakened by distrust, infidelity, deceit and fatigue. I stopped
speaking to him. I could not locate, nor hold in my hands
the language for staying nor for leaving—it fell through my fingers,
like sand.

(Little Indians) A clot the size of my hand birthed itself.
The warm, red blood trickled down my legs. On the floor
in the bathroom, I stared at the flesh I caught in my hands. My fetus'
remains: delicate, pulpy, swirling magentas, sea blue cords, coral
threads.
This ripped my mind into shreds, like a hurricane peels back a metal
roof,
flings what matters most into all directions.

(Ten) I placed the remains onto my ankle-length white cotton
nightgown,
with a trim of a white satin at the hem. I had simple clothes. This one
reminded me of a humble, Mexican table cloth: the kind embroidered
by Indian women. I laid the gown out on my dresser, placed the
bloody,
blue-ish flesh in the front center. It dried overnight to a beautiful plum
brown,
curled into itself like a conch, with a tiny knot at the top, like a tassle.

(Little Indians) I sewed French knots and satin stitch onto my
cotton nightgown, which I'd learned from my friend. I stitched
the first poems I ever wrote with floss, wreathing around the fetal
flesh.

She never asked me about the dried blood. Three months after the
miscarriage,
the gown: shielded with embroidered poems and floss 'drawings':
repressed longing, grief, and pent up rage, became a talisman of all
the losses.
I didn't talk to anyone during this flush of creative energy. After I
finished the last stitch,
I bathed, put on my story-gown, went to the living room, sat on the
couch.
Told my husband of ten years that I was leaving him. He didn't make
a sound.
He just nodded his head.

(Ten) Maura, my five year old daughter, is a fast learner: she begins
to sew two pieces of fabric together: down, push the needle through.
She looks underneath, finds the needle. With the other hand she pulls
the needle through,
looks up at me with surprise and triumph. Eyes shine:
dark chestnut, with skin folds slanted slightly upwards at the outer
corners.
Her small hands try the sequence again. Perfect. She's got it.

(Little Indians) I think back to my mother and aunts: how many
miscarriages . . .
Dismissed as overdue but painful menstrual cycles. And how many
miscarriages my mother had besides the one recorded before my
birth—a boy, my brother. Lost. Disposed of as medical waste at a
hospital in Austin, Texas,
without a ceremonial burial. I claim the wreckage
of my body of his body of the chidrens' bodies
and the toxins consuming us,
and caring for my own dead children,
away from the careless and frigid
systems of hospitals. I see my own denial,
delusions about oil and chemical exposures,
over my own and my mother's lifetimes,
on my body and the bodies of my children.

Margo Tamez

The March

On the way to Hyde park to hear the rally,
Our elbows touched in the street.
I was the woman in the coloured toque and striped scarf
My hooded-top buried under a long wool coat,
The one holding up a sign part of the time—
Well part of the time, till it broke.

I almost didn't see you.
You, the woman, my age, in a wheelchair
Your mom ran over my foot
The wheel stuck on the steel cap of my boot
I wore them just in case there was trouble
Same reason the bandana found a home in my pocket
Ready for the tear gas and too much smoke
Like Seattle or Quebec.

I took your picture.
You, the 3 year old perched on daddy's shoulders
Holding up a home-made sign
Would you bomb me too blazed out in crayon
beside the one make tea not war
Your mum held over your head.

I envied your conviction.
You, the man on crutches
Hobbling through the crowded streets.
How many hours did you keep on walking
Winding your way through London
Adding your voice to the body of the march.

Little girls hung out windows waving scarves
And two windows down a woman sat,
Her cigarette puffing above *Not in my Name*
Stitched in cloth. Vicars marched
Beside pierced men, decorated prams
Carried children into their first memories,
And a shop played love songs through giant speakers
Adding to the roaring wave of the crowd and Sheffield's
Own Samba Band.

I was carried by you.
You, were us, we were 1 million,
1.5, maybe 2 million strong
Who don't want it—I don't want war
But don't have any answers
Know what I don't want
But don't know what to do
So I march and I shout and I question
And I hope it'll give someone, somewhere,
Some time to find some answers
Better than the one we've been given.

Heather Taylor

War Game

(In 2003, the US Army started a business on the side, PlayStation games. Based on military tactics in real war zones, presented as a fictional Middle Eastern country, the first game "US Army" was given out free in shopping malls by recruitment officers. "Full Spectrum Warrior" was produced in 2004, selling quarter of a million copies within two weeks on the market.)

Bill Gates, the boss of Microsoft
can hoist the US flag aloft
because he knows his duty's done –
he's virtually replaced the gun.
From Desert Shield to Desert Storm
technowar's become the norm.
For if the West is where we're from
we get a freebie CD rom.
To play at war without the risk
we need no helmet, just a disc.
The joystick gives an equal joy
to fighting man and playing boy.
"Full Spectrum Warrior" is not
the only game that's getting hot,
for it our fingers have the knack
the "US Army" rocks Iraq.
Filled with awe and hot for shocks
we set our Xbox on the rocks,
then goggle-eyed we twiddle knobs
and slaughter pixellated mobs.
Though Xbox gives the urban oaf a
taste of danger from the sofa,
the mass destruction's digital;
we did not bomb that hospital.
There is no hostile combat zone,
no bleeding baby's fading moan,
no bearded crazy full of hate,
or wedding guest to ventilate.
The server gives us basic training
whilst being highly entertaining.
And though the targets try and try,
it's just a game - we cannot die.

We know the score, but on we plough –
top brass say we are heroes now.
Feel the flesh and hear the screams –
we target practice in our dreams.
The single thing that is a shame
is if we have to stop the game.
Like a junkie with a drug
we hate it if we must unplug.
We only fear a lone attacker –
the fanatical computer hacker.
When a virus eats into our soul
we can't believe we've lost control.
When the VDU disappears,
we're drowning in a nation's tears.
It's just as well it's just pretend,
we'd hate to have to meet our end.
We'd hear no boom, we'd see no flash,
the day our perfect systems crash.

Steve Tasane

Anunci d'una Casa On Ningú No Vol Viure

Catalan

L'han saquejada tants de cops
i gent amb tantes cares
que no hi fa res saber
qui és l'autor dels crims:
podríem ser nosaltres.
Ara només el sol saqueja unes paraules
sense frontisses ni llindars
i enfonsa portes sense pany.

A dins hi viuen dones
plenes de veus que han emmudit
i no saben com estimar-les:
reguen les pedres,
cusen regals per als absents
i t'ofereixen signes,
cendres, pluja del cel.

Escolta'm: sóc l'anunci d'una casa
on ningú no vol viure.
No tens amb què comprar-la: benvingut.

Carles Torner

Ad for the House Where No One Wants to Live

English

They've plundered it so many times,
people with so many faces
it doesn't really matter
who actually committed the crimes:
it could easily be us.
Now only the sun plunders words
with no hinges or thresholds
and knocks down lockless doors.

Inside women live
full of voices grown silent
and they don't know how to love them:
they water stones,
they sew presents for those gone
and they offer you signs,
ashes, rain from the sky.

Heed me: I am the ad for a home
where no one wants to live.
You have nothing to buy it with: welcome.

Translated from the Catalan by D. Sam Abrams
Carles Torner

Response

Yes, the wind does speak
of battles and dreams.
Yes, the currents of the wind take the urgencies
from these mountains.
These mountain ranges have been set on fire
and the flames slice through the televised rhetoric.
Schools become ashes
and churches become empty warehouses.
The exclamations of peace
and freedom
ring
in the ears of crickets.
Yes, bullets do wound the heart and the sky.
And the wind continues speaking
across the leaves of grey trees.

Gustavo Alberto Garcia Vaca

Interrogation

They asked the easy questions first,
like *What is your name?*
So I told them,
but they weren't satisfied.
They wanted a different answer.
Who are you?
I hesitated, then said I didn't know.
They laughed
and said they would torture me
if I didn't improve.
Do you know why you are here?
Because I did something wrong,
I said. They asked me
what that was. I answered
it was because I didn't know.
This time, they didn't laugh.
I was more afraid
and began to tremble. *You are*
a poet? they asked.
I told them I didn't know
what the word meant.
They grew angry. Suddenly,
I was calm. Their hands opened
and closed on the table.
What are your poems worth?
As much as your questions,
I replied.
Their eyes narrowed.
They would detach the skin
from my body, write
along its insides.
Do you know what we can do
to you? Yes,
I answered. And didn't laugh.

Cyril Wong

Occupational Hazards

We all knew that we could get malaria
Hospitals had both patients and mosquitos.

We all knew that we could get tuberculosis
We shared jokes with people who coughed.

We all knew that we could get scabies
We held hands with children who scratched themselves.

We all knew that we could get typhoid
We ate from the same plates.

We all knew that we could get treatment
Quinine, rifampicin, ivermectin, ciprofloxacin.

But nobody ever warned us
That from holding a hand gone limp
From listening to the deafening silence
Of a heart gone quiet
From the tears of a mother
Carrying on into the night

We could catch
Grief.

Ting Hway Wong

Defending God

At the northern end of town
With beards freely flowing
Mallams direct almajiris
And adherents with swords
To slaughter all infidels
Who cannot recite the fatiha.

At the southern end of town
Men, boys and choruses
The church is marching on
With clubs and machetes
To hack down all of the bondwoman
Who cannot say the Lord's prayer.

It is an odd collection
Crosses, crescents and stars,
Tasbis, rosaries and collars,
Modern crusaders and jihadists
With knives, swords, clubs and matchets
Fighting for Allah and Jesus.

Many corpses later
Army tanks roll in
To ensure a cautious mix
On the streets, in offices and markets,
Partners now in hunger and poverty
Fighting for *tuwo, eba* and *amala.*[1]

Waiting, waiting for another time
To defend God.

[1] Basic Nigerian meals from different regions

Kabura Zakama

The President is Dead Again
For Ken Saro-Wiwa and his comrades.

Believe me Mr President General
Some Africans want to die at home

These are not lazy men
These are men of words
The men your people luv
So now boss
Point your guns at your paymaster
And
Shoot,
Take your British arms and
Shoot
Your feet,
Watch your blood and the soil fraternise,
This soil is dead already.

Your corporate friends and city planners have died
Like the soil you killed
They be
Dead, dead, dead
How does it feel to be unburied
Or unincinerated?

President General and friends
Some Africans want to die at home
A natural death
With drummers and the tribe at hand.

A hummingbird tells me dat
Your jails are full of activists
Activists dat are full of life,
The vendor who sold you dat
Pretty, pretty, work of art
And the palace for its comfort
Cannot sell you the silence of the earth community
Or a silent history of your deeds,

Hence I see a day dead Mr President
When your very lovers shall look to earth
Asking
Why?
Look

Look
Check dis
We are watching you,
You do dark we see light
After all,
We are the world.

How many prisoners throats can you cut before you reach hell?
How many children can you stop from growing up?
And remember now
Your business friends will leave you
They will be
Gone,
Gone,
Gone,
Long before your financial returns.

De brothers on de streets who sey respect
Sey no respect
Because yu disrespect
And
A hummingbird tells me dat
Worms are eating you
Before you eat the worms,
You really need to be buried.

Why?
You a warrior wid a poxy mind
Why
Hang your doctor?
And when your death is so wordless
Why send your historians to western capitals?
Listen, listen

Listen to me man
Run, run, run
Find a planet wid no Africa
And act White
De devil will luv you.

Believe me Mr President General
Some Africans want to die at home

Benjamin Zephaniah